Jew for OIL

by

William K. Thornsburg

The Cover: A Ha'apala pastel drawing of an Alyiah Bet sailing ship painted by a child who may well have sailed on board the vessel. The Hebrew writing translates: "A lot of happiness, all good, and immigration soon!!!" This drawing was sold as a rare estate find from a Jewish family album.

ISBN: 978-1-63110-295-0

"I had to do something. A young man came into my home for protection. Is he dangerous? No. Is he a spy? No. Is he a traitor? No. He's just a Jewish teenager who wants to leave." This Righteous Among the Gentiles, and his family, saved over 6,000 Jews.

Chiune Sugihara
Japanese Consul to Lithuania

Introduction

Correspondents and journalists of the armed forces strive to immortalize the saga, temperament, and atrocities of war. World War Two (WWII) was an implacable war of relentless persecution, petty politics, and cowardly mass murders - the daily fares of the life of a Jew. History, especially history clouded in secrecy, reveals the dark side of the human psyche which makes it timeless.

Time, unfortunately, can and does harden the hearts of those who deny the truth and befriend that which is contrary to the welfare of all. The holocaust of WW II did take place. The absence of the holocaust in history books may serve to obscure the evil inclination of man; yet anti-Semitism, empowered by unjustified hatred, survives. The fact remains, due in-part to European pogroms against the Jews and the restrictive, anti-Semitic immigration policies of the nations, the Nazi regime sought to purge the Third Reich and the world of the Jewish race.

On July 31, 1941, the planning of the extermination of "undesirables" began. Two-thirds of the Jewish population, Poles, Romani, Soviet prisoners, Jehovah's Witnesses, homosexuals, and the mentally impaired would succumb to the railways and crematoriums of Auschwitz, Birkenau, and Treblinka - all perpetrated by the free will of man.

What is not recorded within the annals of WWII history, at least not within the realm of Christian journalism, is the plight of Jewish immigration before, during, and after the end of the war – a holocaust within itself; an impregnable "secret" if not for a select few who bore witness to one of the greatest atrocities of WWII. What began on May 13, 1939 on board the German luxury liner *S.S. St. Louis,* ended with the historic voyage of the Zionist ship *Exodus* on July 11, 1947.

The following narrative encompasses 144 ships,[1] and a myriad of smaller vessels, that transported more than 100,000 Jewish immigrants[2] to the shores of Palestine in response to the Nuremberg Laws of 1935, Roosevelt's appalling Evian Conference call to abandon Jewish refugees in 1938, in defiance to the British White Papers of 1939, in opposition to the British-Muslim "Jew for Oil" agreement preventing Jewish refugees throughout WWII and beyond form settling in their homeland.

Jewish immigration carried out in violation of the laws of the governing authority came to be known as independent *Aliyah Bet* in the Zionist lexicon (meaning the clandestine or "illegal" immigration of Jews to Palestine). A significant few of these Aliyah Bet ships have been selected for the following narrative - their passengers and fate having never been formerly acknowledged by war historians.

The governments of Great Britain and the United States advocated anti-Semitic policies that effectively closed the doors to legal immigration and safe havens for thousands of homeless Jews who needlessly perished in the holocaust. These governments further purposed to conceal their clandestine activities against the Aliyah Bet and what transpired aboard their rescue ships. The stories of the following Aliyah Bet ships and private boats are compelling and true, imparted to us by the very individuals who partook of their voyages.

The ships within this narrative are divided into three timeframes: the *Ha'apala* (1935 – 1939), the independent *Aliyah Bet* (1939 – 1945), and the *Bricka* (1945 – 1948), all of which were dedicated to the Zionist Aliyah of illegal immigration to Palestine. Included within their number is a consortium of non-Aliyah Bet "prison" ships whose stories exemplify the unbridled fervor of European anti-Semitism throughout these historic timeframes.

The names David Stoliar, who survived the sinking of the *Struma*, the "dentist of Auschwitz" Benjamin Jacobs, a prisoner on board the *S.S.Cap Arcona*, and "Lady Israel" Ruth Klüger, a Mossad agent who rescued thousands from the hands of Nazis persecutors are forever etched in the chronicles of the Aliyah Bet. It is to their credit, the blood of Bill Bernstein and many others, that the Aliyah Bet Exodus ultimately survived the censorship of history.

May we with one heart purpose to commemorate the loss of those who perished - hundreds of which are still entombed within the hulls of Aliyah Bet vessels. As for the survivors, the resolve of a nation rest in their hands. Their names, once numbered among the damned, are forever counted among the stars of providence.

Many of the Danish ships used to rescue over 7,000 Jewish immigrants from the hands of the Nazis serve as monuments about the shores of Europe. Some have survived, been restored, and rest in museums throughout the world. Some still ply the Adriatic, Black, Mediterranean, and Baltic Seas.

Most (if not all) of the Mossad Aliyah Bet and "illegal" private ships, however, have perished with the passage of time.

Liberties were taken with the following narrative to circumvent the historical data and meritorious genre common among holocaust chronicles. The specific intent of this narrative is to address the clandestine atrocities of the governments of the United States and Great Britain (and her Jewish Agency) that paralleled, or should we say "rivaled" Nazi Germany's indifference towards the European Jews and their right to live where the Almighty G-d ordained for them to live.

If winning the war against Nazi Germany was of primary concern to the United States and Great Britain, then why, having full knowledge of the "Final Solution," did they invest an inordinate amount of military and diplomatic clout to contain the Jews in Europe? Bar the misgivings of saving a few thousand Jews throughout the war, both the American and British governments squandered opportunity after opportunity to provide safe-haven for thousands of fleeing Jews, but instead, bowed down to their almighty quota system and their heathen god of indifference.

Through the efforts of President Harry Truman and Eleanor Roosevelt, that which had previously been vehemently disavowed, that which embodies the very essence of human dignity and national freedom, was finally granted to the Jewish holocaust survivors ... a choice.

Now, ... let us go back in time and relive the past.

Ha'apala

(1935 – 1939)

We begin our narrative with Hitler threatening to annihilate the European Jews if their relocation was not addressed and financed by the American, Soviet, French, and British governments (whose financial kingdoms were all controlled by the Jews). In these perilous times, the Jews sought passage to any safe-haven open to them.

> If the international Jewish financiers in and outside Europe should succeed in plunging the nations once more into a world war, then the result will not be the bolshevization of the earth, and thus the victory of Jewry, but the annihilation of the Jewish race in Europe.[3]
>
> Hitler

In 1934 the first organized efforts at clandestine immigration by sea took place. The Jewish Hehalutz movement chartered the Greek ship *Velos* and, with the aid of Haganah members (a Jewish paramilitary organization), landed some 350 pioneers on the shores of Palestine. Operations were suspended, however, after a second attempt had failed for lack of experience.

The *Velos* chartered by the Hehalutz to rescue 350 Polish refugees in July 1934

5

In 1935, determined to rid Germany of the Jews, Hitler enacted the Nuremberg Laws stripping German Jews of their citizenship and forbidding Jews to marry non-Jewish Germans.[4] The result of these laws was the exclusion of Jews from German social and political life. Jews began to flee by the masses seeking refuge in South America and Palestine. The British White Papers of 1936, written to foster Arab support, restricted Jewish immigration into Palestine. Her Majesty's Royal Navy proceeded to amass a small fleet of war ships and aircraft to prevent Jews from leaving Europe and returning to their G-d-given land at whatever cost and loss of Jewish lives.

It was during this time that the Jewish Revisionist movement, which operate according to its own agenda, established the *Ha'apala* (Jewish "illegal" immigration to Palestine) to facilitate immigration beyond British quotas. Up until the revision of the White Papers in 1939, all "legal" immigration into Palestine was referred to as *Aliyah Alef*; but now, to secure the Arab continued support, the British annulled the Balfour Agreement of WWI and classified all Jews as "enemy aliens" ineligible for a visa to Palestine or anywhere in the British empire.[5]

King David wrote a Psalm (42) about the congregation of Israel, in the midst of her many afflictions, crossing over water to quench her thirst. According to the Jewish Sages, this prophetic psalm about the Jewish exile "was spoken by means of the Holy Spirit, and it expresses the depth of Israel's longing for deliverance."[6] As long as Israel continues in exile, the *Name* of G-d is profaned "and the suffering of Israel is increased because she sorrows at the profanation of His *Name*." The following narrative of the Aliyah Bet during WWII bears witness to this truth.

In 1937, the Revisionists and Betar aliyah youth groups restarted their effort to immigrate to Palestine and in two years sent out several ships, which transported several thousand immigrants from Eastern Europe under the slogan *Af-al-pi* ("in-spite-of..."). Their successful rescue efforts prompted Hehalutz to resume their efforts to rescue "illegal" Jewish immigrants. After the Nazi conquest of Austria and Czechoslovakia, refugee boats were also organized by individual and private organizations.

The Dutch Merchant ship *Poseidon* chartered by the Hehalutz successfully completed two voyages to Palestine in 1938 rescuing a total of 132 Polish refugees

By mid-summer in 1938 some 550,000 Jews were still in Germany and Austria. When the Third Reich annexed Austria in March 1938, the Nazis proceeded to publicly assault Jewish men, women, and even small children while Austrians stood around watching, cheering, and jeering. The Nazis proceeded to round up 200,000 Jews and placed them in concentration camps. The Evian Conference was America's response to Hitler's treatment of European Jews.

Evian Conference

In an effort to deflect attention and criticism from his own national policy that severely limited the quota of Jewish refugees admitted to the United States, in July 1938, President Franklin D. Roosevelt convened a conference of thirty-two "nations of asylum" and the Red Cross in Evian, France to discuss the persecution of the Jews in Europe. The displaced Jewish refugees were in dire need of a safe-haven and "the United States had always been viewed in Europe as a champion of freedom, and with the support of many countries, America's influence could provide the chance to get out of the German trap. The rescue, a new life seemed in reach ..."[7] This was a time when Germany sought every opportunity to rid itself of the Jews. Hitler responded to the news of the conference by saying essentially that if the other nations would agree to take the Jews, he would help them leave.

> I can only hope and expect that the other world, which has such deep sympathy for these criminals [Jews], will at least be generous enough to convert this sympathy into practical aid. We, on our part, are ready to put all these criminals at the disposal of these countries, for all I care, even on luxury ships.[8]
>
> Adolph Hitler

All 32 nations attending the conference (and twenty health organizations) were informed of the horrors perpetrated upon the Jews and the purpose of the conference – to rescue the Jews. On the last day of the conference, the first delegate to speak was the United States Ambassador Myron Taylor whose words reiterated the resolve of the conference (Roosevelt chose not to attend the conference).

Myron began by explaining the quota system of the United States and concluded with a resounding "there is nothing we can do!" ……. then sat down. The Canadian delegate, along with four other delegates, explained that their country could only accept farmers. You had to denounce Judaism and be baptized Christian to go to South America, including the Dominican Republic. The Australian delegate announced that they had no racial problems in Australia and did not want to "import" one. Four of the largest South American countries considered intellectuals and merchants as "undesirables!"[9]

In the end, the 32 nations agreed to make the Virgin Islands a safe haven for the Jews, … BUT Roosevelt and his State Department vehemently opposed their final resolution. Wittingly, Roosevelt succeeded in blocking any safe haven for the Aliyah Bet Jews – the Lord's chosen.

On the opening day of this historic conference, the great *New York Times* ran a small story on page thirteen. Adolf Hitler, in the same paper, was given twice the space about an art show appearance. In fact, few newspapers anywhere in the world addressed the Evian Conference. A small article several days later, on page twenty, celebrated the conference resolution at Evian.[10] America, the most blessed among the Gentile nations, assented to indifference leaving the Jewish "problem" up to G-d.

> At stake at Evian were both human lives – and the decency and self-respect of the civilized world. If each nation at Evian had agreed on that day to take in 17,000 Jews at once, every Jew in the Reich could have been saved.[11]
>
> Walter Mondale

<u>Sando</u>

Prior to WWII, under the oppression of the Romanian Iron Guards (the equivalent of the German SS), the Jews began fleeing Romania from the ports of Constanza and Burgas to Palestine. In March 1939, a private company in Romania ventured to assist the Jewish refugees. A small motor vessel was chartered to transport Austrian and Polish refugees to Palestine. The *Sando* successfully navigated the Danube, the Black Sea, and Mediterranean only to be ambushed by a salvo of British coastal guns off the shores of Palestine. Upon their return to Vienna, they were expelled to Romania and the Iron Guard never to be heard from again.

The 270 Austrian and Polish refugees onboard the *Sando* were the first among many Ha'apala refugees to encounter the crime of British indifference. The *Sando* was eventually captured by the Germans and was at their service between 1941 and 1942. There were many refugee ships to follow, piloted by crews who often sacrificed the loss of their ship and/or their lives. No doubt these crews had families of their own. Perhaps the most successful of these aliyah ships was the Hehalutz ship *Atrato*.

<u>S.S. Atrato</u>

The *Atrato* of Greek registry was a relatively light boat, fast and easy to sail, but it was not designed for human cargo – especially in great quantities. Previously, she was used as a cargo ship by the Russian Navy and continued to serve the Ha'apala, carrying human cargo on seven different voyages from ports in Italy, Romania, and Bulgaria – the most number of voyages by any aliyah ship.

On her first voyage, the *Atrato* unloaded her 300 refugees on the Palestine beach who, subsequently, were herded up by the British police. The refugees were confined on the beach for a week until Haganah soldiers arrived and freed them. On her sixth voyage, however, the *Atrato* was fired upon by a British police boat as she approached the Palestine coast. One refugee was killed before the ship could turn away. On her seventh voyage, she was captured by the British navy. The ship was confiscated, and her passengers were placed in the British Atlit concentration camp in Palestine.

From November 1938 to May 1939, a total of 2,450 refugees from Poland, Germany, and Austria made their way to Palestine on board the *Atrato*. What an undertaking this must have been. The Hehlutz, an independent aliyah group supported by the Mossad (operating arm of the Haganah), provided for the ship and all the provisions for the seven voyages with the loss of only one refugee.

The salvage vessel *Atrato* built in 1899 was chartered by Hehlutz to rescue 2,450 immigrants from Yugoslavia

During the Ha'apala movement, some 30 plus Mossad ships were able to successfully transport thousands of Jewish

11

refugees to the shores of Palestine without being detected. Easy access to ships and crews strengthened the resolve of what was to become known as the Aliyah Bet stage of illegal immigration.

Dora

On the morning of Sunday, July 16, 1939, the *Dora*, a small coal/cattle ship with "slave quarters," sailing under Panamanian flag, left the harbor of Amsterdam (Netherlands) with 300 Jewish refugees. The Dutch government, sympathetic towards the Jews, turned a blind eye and let them leave secretly.

The *Dora*, a strong and stable vessel, was purchased in Copenhagen, Denmark by the Mossad. They installed 175 iron bunk beds, a kitchen, lavatories, and showers, cleaned the motors, and acquired lifebelts for the passengers. Working in conjunction with the Mossad, another 180 members of the Hehalutz joined them in Antwerpen, Belgium.

S.S. Dora, the "Coffin Ship"

By a stroke of luck (or divine intervention) the British allowed the ship through the strait of Gibraltar believing that "illegal" immigrants never came through the straight but instead from the French Riviera, the Italian coast, and the coast of the Black Adriatic Sea. Consequently, the *Dora,* the first aliyah voyage to leave from a Northern European harbor, successfully disembarked its refugees on the coast of Palestine during the night of August 11.

The story of the German liner *M.S. St. Louis* proved to be one the most shameful accounts of Christian indifference towards the Lord's people, and unfortunately, was the first of many to follow.

M.S. St. Louis

Up until the beginning of WWII on September 1, 1939, the immigration policies of these thirty-two "nations of asylum" made it exceedingly difficult for Jews to flee from the Nazi regime. During this time, empowered by the Evian Resolution, Hitler orchestrated a diabolical plan to reiterate the fact that "no nation" welcomed the Jews. Those who possessed the necessary finances and documentation, including those interned in concentration camps, boarded one of the finest German luxury liners and set sail for Cuba on May 13, 1939.

The *M.S. St Louis* was a beautiful ship with luxurious ballrooms and swimming pools of which the Jewish children were not accustomed. Aboard the *St. Louis* were 932 refugees, most of which possessed affidavits or registration numbers for immigration into the United States.

Many of the passengers were men who had relinquished all to purchase a passage to America with the hopes of bringing their families over at a later date. They had no other option, leave or return to the concentration camps. Two weeks later, the *St. Louis* dropped anchor at the far end of Havana Harbor.

M.S. St. Louis entering Havana Harbor in 1939.

Prior to the arrival of the *St. Louis*, twenty-three Ha'alapa ships had successfully transported 1,740 Jewish refugees to South American countries. The Cuban government allowed 22 non-Jewish passengers to disembark but denied entry for the remaining 915 refugees. Anti-Semitism and greedy politicians circumvented human dignity and compassion.

Captain Gustav Schröder of the *St. Louis,* subsequently, set sail for the United States having earlier requested from the government of the U.S. permission to disembark the Jewish children on board his ship. For three days, escorted by a U.S. Coast Guard cutter with aerial support, he waited for a response, but none came.[12] Next he tried the Canadian Prime Minister who also rejected his entreaties: "none is too many!"[13] responded his immigration officer.[14] Schröder's request to disembark his passengers in the Dominican Republic, Shanghai or anywhere else was also denied. Consequently, Hitler ordered Schröder to return to Germany.

Photo of *St. Louis* passengers, many would later perish at the hands of indifference.

When the Dominican Republic made a public offer to take in 100,000 Jews on visas, the Roosevelt administration undermined the plan. From Roosevelt's point of view, "that country was too close to home, and Jews deposited there would inevitably come to America." Officials in the US Virgin Islands, too, were willing to rescue Jews by letting them into the country, but Roosevelt again halted the plan.[15]

Due to the heroic efforts of Captain Schröder and the American Jewish Joint Distribution Committee (JDC), several European nations would eventually accept the remaining refugees on board the beleaguered *St. Louis* (254 of which would later perish at the hands of Nazi Germany). Sadly, Roosevelt's indifference only hastened Hitler's final solution.

The book *Voyage of the Damned* written by Gordon Thomas in 1974 and the film release in 1976 is based on eyewitness accounts of the 1939 voyage of the *St. Louis* cruise ship. There are those who question Captain Schröder's intentions for entering U.S. waters yet fail to address why President Roosevelt and the State Department turned a deaf ear to Jewish immigration both prior to, during, and after the war.

Three months before the *St. Louis* sailed, Congressional leaders in both U.S. houses allowed to die, in committee, a rescue/immigration bill sponsored by Senator Robert Wagner and Representative Edith Rogers. Senator Robert Reynolds countered the bill calling upon Congress to abolish all Jewish immigration for the next 10 years. Roosevelt's only action was "file-no action."[16] This bill would have admitted 20,000 Jewish children from Germany above the existing quotas.[17] Throughout the war thousands of British children were admitted into the US without visas of their own ... the only stipulation was they could not be an endangered Jewish child!

Must we forget that there was a real labor shortage in America throughout the war – a labor shortage that would employ several hundred thousand German POW's and Mexican immigrants as farm and factory workers; yet the U.S. Congress could find no room for well-educated, highly productive Jewish laborers.

The German POW camps in America were equipped with facilities and services that could be found in a small town - dentists, doctors, libraries, movies, educational facilities, and athletics. Some of the Nazi prisoners (officers) were placed in private housing and apartments furnished with cars and personal drivers.[18] Is it any wonder that many of these POWs chose to stay in America after the war and were granted citizenship with open arms by Congress?

Mind you, the *St. Louis* affair was only the beginning of what lay in store for the homeless Jew. Quite independent and calculating was the demonization and deliberation of the Jewish people by the Allied powers - Great Britain and its Jewish Agency Zionists, and the United States. All was done in secrecy, seasoned in arrogance and willful effacement of the human spirit – a pogrom of dire consequences for all who flout *the fear of the Lord.*

Flandre

Two other ships arrived at the Havana Harbor in May 1939 carrying Jewish refugees, the British ship *Orduña* carrying 55 Jewish refugees, and the French ship *Flandre* carrying 104 refugees. Both ships had regular cruises to South American ports and had deposited hundreds of passengers over the previous five years. Neither ship, however, was allowed to disembark their Jewish refugees; once again, those carrying their U.S. immigration documents, without further explanation, were not allowed to negotiate their worth.

The French liner *Flandre* at the Havana dock in 1939.

The *Orduña* refugees, with the help of the JDC and a New York based Hebrew Immigration Aid Society, would eventually immigrate to the United Stated. The 104 Jewish refugees on board the *Flandre*, however, were shipped back to France and sent directly to Nazi death camps.[19] Roosevelt and his State Department simply could not find the time or the space for 104 fleeing refugees to America. Although the quota for German immigration into the U.S. had not reduced, the American officials threw up a bureaucratic wall to limit "Jewish" immigration by extending the acquisition time of Jewish visas by several years – virtually closing the doors to Jewish immigration.

M.S. Orinoco

A few days after the *St. Louis* incident, the *M.S. Orinoco* with 200 Jewish refugees aboard, set sail for Cuban waters. Informed by radio of the difficulties in Havana, the captain of the *Orinoco* diverted the ship to waters just off Cherbourg, France, where it remained for several days. The Cuban treatment of the *St. Louis* refugees, and to a lesser extent of those aboard the *Flandre* and *Orduña*, had focused international scrutiny on Cuba's immigration procedures. Nevertheless, neither the British nor the French government was prepared to accept the *Orinoco's* homeless refugees.

M.S. Orinoco
in 1939

The United States government intervened, but halfheartedly. U.S. diplomats in London pressured the German ambassador to give assurances that the German authorities would not persecute the *Orinoco* refugees upon their return to the German Reich. With this dubious assurance, at the insistence of President Roosevelt, the 200 refugees were shipped back to Germany in June 1939.[20] Their fate remains unknown – at least none have yet to come forth and tell their story.

Captain Schröder (*M.S. St. Louis*) had included "Shanghai" (China) as a possible home of disembarkation for his Jewish refugees. Indeed, Shanghai had offered an open door to refugees for nearly a century before Jewish refugees began to arrive in large numbers at the end of 1938. Shanghai, now under the control of the Japanese, was an open city and did not have visa restrictions on immigration. As of yet, the Japanese had not entered the war as an Axis power, and, having not received an open invitation to attend the Evian Conference, was neither bound by the Evian Resolution nor indulged in trifle hypocrisy. The Japanese, fully aware of Germany's anti-Semitic posture, possessed the resources and uncompromising resolve to rescue the Jews – and they did (throughout the war), much to the consternation of the U.S., Great Britain, and France.

In 2009, the 111th Congress unanimously approved Senate Resolution 111 formerly "acknowledging the suffering of the *St. Louis* refugees caused by the refusal of the United States, Cuban, and Canadian governments to provide them political asylum."[21] May this Resolution also apply to the refugees aboard the refuge ships *Flandre*, *Orduña,* and the

SENATE RESOLUTION 111

Recognizing June 6, 2009, as the 70th anniversary of the tragic date when the M.S. St. Louis, a ship carrying Jewish refugees from Nazi Germany, returned to Europe after its passengers were refused admittance to the United States.

Whereas on May 13, 1939, the ocean liner M.S. St. Louis departed from Hamburg, Germany for Havana, Cuba with 937 passengers, most of whom were Jewish refugees fleeing Nazi persecution;

Whereas the Nazi regime in Germany in the 1930s implemented a program of violent persecution of Jews;

Whereas the Kristallnacht, or Night of Broken Glass, pogrom of November 9 through 10, 1938, signaled an increase in violent anti-Semitism;

Whereas after the Cuban Government, on May 27, 1939, refused entry to all except 28 passengers on board the M.S. St. Louis, the M.S. St. Louis proceeded to the coast of south Florida in hopes that the United States would accept the refugees;

Whereas the United States refused to allow the M.S. St. Louis to dock and thereby provide a haven for the Jewish refugees;

Whereas the Immigration Act of 1924 placed strict limits on immigration;

Whereas a United States Coast Guard cutter patrolled near the M.S. St. Louis to prevent any passengers from jumping to freedom;

Whereas following denial of admittance of the passengers to Cuba, the United States, and Canada, the M.S. St. Louis set sail on June 6, 1939, for return to Antwerp, Belgium with the refugees; and

Whereas 254 former passengers of the M.S. St. Louis died under Nazi rule.

Orinoco all of which were diverted from the American shores in strict adherence to U.S. immigration policy. Three hundred refugees from these ships ended up in German extermination camps.

Sadly ... there is more, much more to this saga. The holocaust and Allied indifference toward the Jews were mutually exclusive events – both of which sanctioned the persecution and slaughter of innocent Jews.

S.S. Hikawa Maru

The obvious and desirable destination for Jewish immigration was impossible. Immigration to Palestine had already been severely reduced by the British in 1936, and by 1939, the "White Papers" effectively closed Palestine to legal Jewish entry.[22] Furthermore, the Kristallnacht and Lithuanian "Christian" pogroms (organized massacre of the Jews) of 1938 and 1939 added several hundred thousand Jews to the already growing number of nationless Jews – not to mention the 1.5 million Jewish women and children slaughtered by the merciless Ukrainian population!

S.S.Hikawa Maru

Had it not been for the heroic efforts of two foreign diplomats Chinese Consul-General Ho Feng-Shan[23] and the

Japanese Vice-Consul Chiune Sugihara who circumvented political quandaries and issued thousands of visas to Jewish refugees, many of the German, Polish, Austrian, and Lithuanian Jews would not have survived the holocaust (Sugihara saved 6,000 alone!).[24] Many were transported to New York (the present Orthodox communities) with forged Japanese passports and visas on board the Japanese ocean liners *S.S. Hikawa Maru, S.S. Hakone Maru, S.S. Hakusan Maru,* and the *S.S. Kashima Maru.*

Using Italian and Japanese ships, Ho and Chiune rescued 1,000 Jewish refugees a month transporting most of them to Shanghai. Once on board these Italian and Japanese cruise ships, the refugees were treated equally with other passengers and crew, were not placed in barbed-wire cages, were well fed, and were not subject to exorbitant ticket prices – tickets that otherwise could not have been acquired. Many of the refugees were traveling as families and all survived the war.

Apart from the Ha'apla, Jewish refugees took advantage of luxury liners that visited the ports of Genoa and Trieste, Italy. Some notable liners are recorded within this narrative whose stories exemplify the chaos and hardships refugees encountered and the despicable acts of those who attempted to keep the Jews confined in Nazi Europe.

Conte Verde

Central European Jews appeared in large numbers in Shanghai because they were not wanted in the West. The

Asian governments of China and Japan did not foster religious, racial, and cultural prejudices against Jews, which were prevalent America and Europe. These were ordinary Jews, not the wealthy and famous whose lives have often been retold. The Shanghai Jews had nobody to vouch for them in the U.S., were unable to bring significant financial resources out of the Third Reich and had no especially desirable skills. The Italian ship *Conte Verde* was one of four cruise ships the Italians used to transport Jewish refugees to Shanghai. The Lloyd Trieste Line transported more refugees than Canada, Australia, New Zealand, South Africa, and India combined[25] and at a fraction of the cost of most private rescue ships.

S.S. Conte Verde of the Italian Lloyd Trieste Line. There were three other Lloyd Trieste ships that ferried Jewish refugees to Shanghai: the sister ship *S.S. Conte Rosso,* the *S.S. Conte Biancamano,* and the *S.S. Conte Grande.*

Shanghai was a capitalist paradise. Two large sections of central Shanghai became autonomous foreign entities; the International Settlement dominated by British-American business interests and governed by the Shanghai Municipal Council (SMC), and the French Concession, run by the French government through its Consul General. Nestled within the Old Shanghai section was a small Jewish settlement of approximately five thousand Baghdadi Sephardic and Russian Ashkenazi refugees who had earlier fled the Russian pogroms and Revolution of 1917. Aided by the JDC, these Shanghai Jews bore the burden of hosting an influx of some 20,000 Jewish refugees. This figure may have increased dramatically had it not been for the intervention of the U.S. and British governments.

The Westerners in Shanghai had everything, yet their collective reaction to the appearance of the *Conte Verde,* carrying penniless refugees from Nazi Germany, was to prevent any more from landing. The Vice Chairman of the SMC made this painfully clear stating that "the Council must not take any action which can possibly be interpreted to mean that it is, or ever will be, in any way responsible for the maintenance of the [Jewish] refugees in question."[26]

JDC kitchen in Shanghai feeding 8,500 refugees twice a day.

A more restrictive immigration policy was demanded by the American, British, and French businessmen who were in charge of the settlement sections in Shanghai. Economic self-interest and traditional anti-Semitism determined the hostile reaction of Shanghai's Western elite. The SMC, fully aware of German hostilities towards the Jews, demanded of the Japanese to prevent the arrival of any further Jewish refugees; a demand the Japanese Foreign Ministry refused to comply.[27]

In December 1938, Washington and London, continuing to prioritize the economic advantage of their citizens in Shanghai over the lives of foreign Jews, officially requested the Nazis not to allow any further Jews to leave Germany for Shanghai.[28] In May 1939, with 2,000 Jews arriving every month, the Japanese, with Berlin's approval, announced that no further refugees would be admitted into Shanghai after August 21, 1939. Although these new regulations did not specifically mention the Jews, it was clear that only refugees with a "J" stamped into their passports would be affected.

The SMC followed with their own decree that European refugees would no longer be permitted to enter the International Settlement. All this was accomplished by the U.S. and Great Britain knowing full well that Shanghai was a vital, if not the last, safe-haven for the ill-fated "Evian Conference" Jew.

Let us not forget that during this time the British had been actively engaged, since 1936, in accosting any Ha'apala refugee ship that dare seek safe-haven in its own country much less in China. And, once again, we find the U.S. collaborating with Nazi Germany on the containment of Jews in Germany and its occupied nations. Fortunately, the humanitarian intervention of Italian and Japanese rescue ships effectively promulgated the necessity of a Jewish State and saved thousands of Jewish refugees from the anti-Semitic immigration policies of the United States and Great Britain – at least for the time being.

After Japan declared war on the United States in 1941, Nazi Germany assumed Japan would implement a "Final Solution in Shanghai" or adopt the Joseph Meisinger Plan (the "Butcher of Warsaw"). One section of the plan called for placing "Jewish refugees in old ships and setting them adrift on the East China Sea, so that they would eventually die of hunger"[29] – a policy sanctioned by the Royal Navy throughout the war to combat Jewish "illegal" immigration into Palestine.[30] The Gestapo was dispatched to Shanghai.

Japanese Foreign Minister Matsuoka stated, "I am the man responsible for the alliance with Hitler, but nowhere have I promised that we would carry out his anti-Semitic policies in Japan. This is not simply my personal opinion, it is the opinion of Japan, and I have no compunction about announcing it to the world."[31]

The Japanese officials, unequivocally, found the Meisinger Plan both intellectually and emotionally unacceptable. With the intercession of the Shanghai Rabbi, Amshenower Regge, and the translation skills of Leo (Ariyeh) Hanin, the Japanese ultimately defied the German Gestapo and protected the Jews of Shanghai throughout the war.[32] The personal accounts of those who sailed to Shanghai on board the *Conte Verde* are detailed in *Exodus to Shanghai* by Steve Hochstadt.

The reason why Captain Schöder was denied passage to Shanghai, with his 915 Jewish refugees on board the *St. Louis,* can be directly attributed to the SMC's anti-Semitism and self-interests in Shanghai. The actions of the SMC not only sealed the fate of 254 refugees aboard the *St. Louis* (who eventually perished at the hands of the Nazis), it indirectly sanctioned Hitler's "Final Solution" by preventing a great number of European Jews from escaping genocide.

As of 2015, neither the governments of the U.S. or Great Britain, nor the French government has expressed any remorse whatsoever for their callus and premeditated treatment of homeless human beings in Shanghai.

Fortunately, a "sister" refugee camp of Shanghai refugees flourished in the Philippines, all of which survived the war. Most of the refugees were transported to the Philippines on board the German liner *Scharnhorst*.

S.S. Scharnhorst

In 1934 the Hapag-Lloyd shipping company launched the first of three "East Asia Express Steamers" capable of attracting continental traffic away from the dominant foreign companies. The luxurious steamer *S.S. Scharnhort* and her sister ship *S.S. Gneisenau* ran the Asian express transporting thousands of European refugees from Baltic and Mediterranean ports to Asian destination, including Shanghai. The *Scharnhorst* was one of the last ships to leave the Shanghai port with Jewish refugees on board. The destination of her passengers was a relatively unknown haven in the Pacific Ocean.

In May 15, 1939, The *Scharnhorst* arrived in Manila - a U.S. Commonwealth in the Pacific. European Jews for the past two years were migrating to Asian ports such as Bangkok, Singapore, Hong Kong, and Manila – especially Manila. The Philippine President Manual Quezon and the U.S. High Commissioner Paul McNutt established the Jewish Relief Committee (JRC) to provide financial funding and jobs for Shanghai transfers.

The *S.S. Scharnhorst*
Built in Bremen,
Germany
Length: 626 ft.

This small Jewish community had a synagogue, a Rabbi, a Cantor, and a Woman's Auxiliary. Jewish life in Manila flourished. With the outbreak of war in Europe in 1939, *Scharnhorst* was caught in the Orient and was unable to return to Germany. In February 1942, the ship was sold to Japan and was taken over by the Imperial Japanese Navy. She was moved to the naval yard at Kure and converted to an escort carrier – the *Shinyo* (the "Godly Hawk"). On November 17, 1944, *Shinyo* was torpedoed and sank.

Jewish refugees in Manila celebrating Passover.

It is remarkable how one small nation in the Far East managed to do what the U.S. and Great Britain were reluctant to do – save Jewish lives. High Commissioner McNutt was able to circumvent the State Department obstructions to Jewish rescue and more than quadrupled the Jewish population of Manila. President Quezon donated his land to accommodate the influx of 1,300 Shanghai refugees, all of whom survived the brutal Japanese occupation of the Philippines.

There are many more ships and stories to explore, most of which defy imagination. Unfortunately, the anti-Semitic immigration policies of the U.S. and Great Britain and their influence around the globe ran their course throughout WWII preventing thousands from escaping the death camps of Nazi Germany.

* * *

From here we enter into the second stage of Jewish "illegal" immigration to Palestine – called the *Aliyah Bet*. This stage of the Ha'apala movement, in violation of British White Paper restrictions of 1939, encompasses the "Final Solution," more anti-Semitic pogroms against the European Jews, the US-British restrictive policies against Jewish immigration, and the commercialization of Jewish souls. Hitler, Roosevelt, and Churchill were committed to appeasing the Arab nations by restricting Jewish access to their promised, G-d given land – a "Jew-for-oil" exchange.

Oil, the "G-d" of America and Great Britain, was subsidized with Jewish blood. Hitler and his Arab supporter, the Grand

Mufti (who provoked pogroms in Palestine in 1929 killing over 500),[33] were both committed to the uncompromising war against the Jews – a war that included the murder of over six million Jews and countless more innocent victims. Nurtured and strengthened by British and American anti-Semitic policies, the Hitler-Mufti alliance proved to be the most unholy, barbaric alliance of the twentieth century dedicated to the destruction of the Jewish people.

Furthermore, the very nations that agreed to support the State of Israel have since sought to take away their land, speak haughty words against the Jew, and honor all who dishonor the *Name* of G-d, or at least pay no heed to scripture (Joel 3:2) where the Lord specifically identifies Israel as "my people." The truth of the matter is that the nations of the world do not fear the G-d of Israel, and when they sin, they blame the Jews, enact pogroms against those they hate, and "defile the *Name* of G-d" with their ungodly deeds! This has been going on for centuries. And what did G-d say to Abraham: *"I will bless them that bless thy seed [plural, generations to come]and curse him that curseth thee."*[34]

As we have witnessed over and over again throughout the Jewish scriptures, the G-d of the Jew invariably summons an insignificant number of individuals (the "Aliyah Bet Shipping Company") to fight and overcome great odds for the glory of His Holy *Name*! The *Aliyah Bet* is truly a remarkable narrative about a most remarkable people.

The aliyah ships within this movement are many yet none are without significance. The private motor craft and small boats used to support larger vessels are also varied and numerous - all of which played a major role in the Aliyah Bet rescue of Jewish refugees. With the financial assistance of the JDC, private, and Mossad run organizations, the refugees were transported by various means in Aliyah Bet ships. Those who sought out private ships, however, paid exorbitant amounts for their fares and were often dismayed with what they had bargained for. Get rich schemes abounded with little thought as to the well-being or safety of their Jewish clients.

We need also mention that during this time period, the German military and refugees, fleeing the advancement of the Red Army, paid dearly for the atrocities of their government. The sinking of the transport ship *Wilhelm Gustloff,* in January 1945, carrying over 10,000 wounded soldiers, German officers and their families, was the greatest maritime disaster in history! Among the dead (three times that of the *Titanic* and *Lusitania* combined) were 4,000 infant children.

As with most of the Aliyah Bet stories and British maritime atrocities of WWII, the sinking of the *Wilhelm Gustloff*, the *HMT Lancastria* transport liner (9,000 lives lost), the Russian hospital ship *Armenia* (7,000 lives lost), the German liner *Goya* (7,000 lives lost), have somehow eluded our remembrance.

Aliyah Bet

(1939 – 1945)

Prior to the advent of the 1939 White Papers, most Zionist organizations dedicated to the resumption of Jewish sovereignty in the Land of Israel, preferred to support legal immigration to Palestine (referred to as *Aliyah Alef*). From May 23, 1939 on, however, the Mossad took charge of the "illegal" immigration to Palestine (called the *Aliyah Bet*).

On June 27, 1941 one of many Christian pogroms against Jews took place in Lasi, Romania. The massacre of Jews by the populace of Lasi included 8,000 the first day - prior to the death train murders. In the death train that left Iaşi for Călăraşi, southern Romania, which carried perhaps as many as 5,000 Jews, only 1,011 reached their destination alive after seven days. (The Romanian police counted 1,258 bodies, yet hundreds of dead were thrown out of the train on the way at Mirceşti, Roman, Săbăoani, and Inoteşti.) The death train to Podu Iloaiei (15 kilometers from Iaşi) had up to 2,700 Jews upon departure, of which only 700 disembarked alive. In the official account, Romanian authorities reported that 1,900 Jews boarded the train and 'only' 1,194 died."[35]

Throughout 1940 and 1942, in concert with Nazi Germany, anti-Semitic pogroms in Poland, Romania, Ukraine, and

Lithuania, orchestrated by civilians as well as the militaries of European nations, massacred thousands of Jewish citizens – 170,000 in Romania alone![36] The madness in which these nations butchered their Jewish neighbors is incomprehensible. Such hatred against the Jews by the Poles, Czechs, Hungarians, Romanians, Austrians, Ukrainians, and Lithuanians beaconed the call of the *Aliyah Bet* fleet.

The rich oilfields in the Middle East were a source of contention throughout WWII. Both Hitler and the British aggressively sought the Arab alliance pledging to keep the Jews out of Palestine - the "Jew for Oil" agreement.[37] Fearing an Arab reprisal, totally insensitive to the holocaust of European Jews, the British abandoned their 1917 Balfour Declaration that endorsed the establishment of a Jewish State in Palestine; furthermore, they declared war on Jewish refugees and there *Aliyah Bet* rescue ships.

Ships purchased or chartered during this stage of the *Aliyah Bet*, were hard to find, very expensive, rickety, unseaworthy ships devoid of amenities, crammed 5 to 10 times their normal capacities, and their destiny was, in most cases, fatal. During the latter part of 1938 through 1939 many refugee ships set out from ports in Yugoslavia and Romania or further up the Danube.

Aliyah Bet refugees that found their way to the Black Sea and sailed the Mediterranean were captured, resisted arrest, were beaten and killed by their British captors. Once contained, the refugees were either set adrift at sea without food, water, and fuel never to be seen again, sent back to their Nazi aggressors, or were counted against the Palestine quotas[38] and confined to British concentration camps in Palestine, Cyprus, or Mauritius.

Over 25 *Aliyah Bet* ships and a number of smaller vessels were conscripted during this timeframe. Several of these ships made multiple voyages. There were also several non-*Aliyah Bet* ships whose stories serve to illustrate the pre-war and post-war anti-Semitism that pervaded most European countries, especially in the United Kingdom. In fact, this second stage of the *Alyiah Bet* begins with a horrific example of anti-Semitic brutality aboard a non-*Alyiah Bet* ship – the *HMT Dunera*. Our narrative begins during the summer of 1940, soon after the fall of France.

HMT Dunera

After the fall of France, 2,542 men of German and Austrian origin, in Britain, were rounded up as a precaution. The intention had been to segregate those who might pose a risk to British security from those who were neutral. These "enemy aliens" consisted of 200 Italian and 251 German prisoners of war along with 2,036 Jewish refugees ages 16 through 60 (including 800 survivors of the sinking of the British prison ship *Arandora Star* on 2 July 1940). Some of these refugees were displaced "Kindertransport" children rescued earlier from Nazi tyranny and sent to the United Kingdom before the outbreak of WWII.

Prior to boarding the *Dunera*, the Jews were stripped of precious items including jewelry, money, false teeth, vital medicines, insulin, valuable documents, immigration visas identifying them as Jews, testimonials of every sort, most of which were thrown on the ground or simply torn up. The "enemy aliens" were summarily herded aboard a troop carrier built for 1,600 and headed for Sydney, Australia.

HMT Dunera

"The ship was an overcrowded Hell-hole. Hammocks almost touched, many men had to sleep on the floor. Water and food was rationed and toilet facilities were totally inadequate."[39] Because of the severe overcrowding, the men were confined to the dark, dirty, stifling hot hull. The portholes were secured throughout most of the voyage and the air vents were kept closed and rarely, during their voyage, were the men allowed to go topside for fresh air.

Braving the whims of the guards, the Jews took turns topside. They were required to walk barefoot on decks covered in shattered glass. Many were belittled, beaten with rifle butts, and bayonetted. Dysentery ran through the ship. They had no change of clothing for their luggage had previously been thrown overboard or kept locked up.[40] One particular prisoner, on the day his Argentina visa expired, leaped into the sea. He had previously informed other prisoners that both his father and grandfather had committed suicide by jumping over a ship's side.

The men had previously signed papers stating that their families, on convoy ships, would meet them in Canada when, in fact, the *Dunera* disembarked in Australia. Prior to their arrival, the *Dunera* was graced with two torpedoes that grazed the side of the hull. Only one prisoner, other than the suicide, perished during the trip – a Jewish refugee.

Upon arrival in Sydney, an Australian medical officer examined the pale and emaciated condition of the prisoners. His subsequent report led to the court martial of several of the crew members including the senior officer. "The sentences meted out to them were hardly commensurate with their misdeeds and brutality."[41] The enemy aliens were subsequently transported by train to a rural town in New South Wales where the Australian soldiers graciously catered to their every need.

Winston Churchill (not the British Royalty) accepted full responsibility for such inhumane treatment of human beings, would later describe the *Dunera* affair as "a deplorable and regrettable mistake."[42] In all, 7,000 enemy aliens were shipped overseas to Canada and Australia including some 400 Kindertransport children. Most were treated decently, the experience aboard the *Dunera* being the exception.

The *Dunera* Affair, nevertheless, epitomizes man's wanton indulgence of his sinful inclination – that of hatred and indifference. Such was not limited to this one incident but was gainfully manifested throughout the Royal Navy's treatment of holocaust refugees aboard the myriad of Aliyah Bet rescue ships.

<u>S.S. Pentcho</u>

The Danube River, flowing from the middle of Europe to the Black Sea, was an international waterway that could be traversed by Jewish refugees without travel documents of any kind, provided shipping was obtainable; for a price, it usually was. The Danube was also used by the Nazis to transport Jews from Romania, Yugoslavia, and Hungary to the death camps. Needless to say, it was a life-threatening experience for a Jew to traverse the Danube.

Not counting a multitude of small craft that remain mostly unaccounted for and probably lost at sea, there were 34 "illegal" sea voyages originating in the Danube from the end of 1937 until the outbreak of the war; thereafter, there were another 28, the last of them in August 1944. Most were sponsored by Zionists groups (principally the Revisionists and the Mossad). The story of the *Pentcho* is perhaps the most exhilarating voyage of them all.

The New Zionist Organization (NZO) was one of the first groups, after the fall of France, to acquire *Aliyah Bet* ships. This particular Revisionist group was led by leaders of the Jewish youth movement called *Betar* whose first mission was to rescue 280 Slovakian Jews stranded in Prague. The voyage of this Betar ship exemplifies the endurance, risks and hardships Aliyah Bet refugees undertook to escape both British tyranny and the death camps of Nazi Germany.

Twice the small group of Betar refugees had purchased a ship to embark down the Danube, through the Black Sea, the Aegean and eastern Mediterranean Sea on their long journey to Palestine. Twice their ships were diverted to assist the urgent needs of other European refugees. Finally, a NZO agent was summoned from Bratislava to inspect a riverboat lying in the Danube port of Braila, Romania and determine if the vessel was seaworthy and could accommodate the Slovak contingent.

Registered in Naples, the *Stefano* was a side-wheel paddle steamer of dubious condition, uncertain age and even more uncertain provenance that had been plying the lower reaches of the Danube since the turn of the century. It was 165 feet long and 40 feet wide with a mere five-foot draft … and no one in his right mind would consider going to sea in this old cattle boat! Nevertheless, the Slovak group had been waiting for their ship since September 1938.

It was now December 1938, the Danube was frozen, and Nazis persecution was on the rise. The *Stefano* was purchased for $30,000 dollars, refitted for 300 passengers, registered as the *Pentcho* under the Bulgarian flag, and set sail for Bratislava.

The *Pentcho* was a converted 165 ft. cattle boat with a draft of only 5 feet.

Many daunting challenges lay ahead of the voyage, most notable; this cargo vessel had never been allowed above a point known as the Iron Gate near the Romanian-Yugoslavian border because her hull could not withstand the swift currents which flowed there.

A superstructure had to be constructed giving the *Pentcho* three sleeping levels – one in the cargo hold whose occupants would serve as human ballast, one just below the deck, and one inside the topside superstructure. Toilets and washrooms were built between these living spaces. Each sleeping space measured 2 feet 6 inches wide by 5 feet 3 inches long, with only two feet of headroom. By the time the *Pentcho* set sail, another 100 passengers arrived bringing the total, including crew, to just over 400.

Any vessel departing Vienna and Bratislava was monitored by the Royal Navy. Every effort was made by British officials to prevent Jewish refugees from using the Danube as an escape corridor. Prior to their departure on May 1940, the British government pressed the Hungarians and Bulgarians to prevent the *Pentcho* and any other refugee laden ship from escaping Germany.[43] Such was the resolve of the British to prevent Jewish refugees from escaping European persecution - the Jew for Oil agreement.

The *Pentcho,* piloted by a White Russian, morphine addict with one leg, spent four months navigating the Danube - a voyage upon whose borders lay a host of hostile, pro-Nazi countries. The maritime commissioners upon boarding the *Pentcho* were astounded at the deplorable condition of the ship. The engine was clogged with years of hardened grease and steam leaking from the boiler pipes. The sleeping quarters were inundated with bedbugs coupled with an all-apparent infestation of lice. Indeed, the life aboard the *Pentcho* was deplorable; so was the case with most of the Aliyah Bet ships.

The Yugoslavian commissioners moored the *Pentcho* for six weeks at the dangerous Kazan Defile fearing the *Pentcho* would sink and block commercial navigation. During this time, the *Pentcho* picked up another 101 refugees released from the Dachau concentration camp, bringing the total on board the *Pentcho* to 514. The Yugoslavian government would eventually assent, latch two barges onto the *Pentcho*, and towed the ship safely through the Defile. Finally, on September 14, the *Pentcho* reached the seaport of Sulina, Romania. The Betar leader, having promised the passengers that a sea-going ship would transfer them to Palestine once they reached the Black Sea, informed the passengers that no such ship existed. To escape Nazi aggression, they had to leave immediately.

Somehow, by the grace of G-d, the paddleboat survived the tempest of the Black Sea, sailed to the Athens port of Piraeus in the Aegean Sea and picked up supplies. Three days after they left Piraeus, two Italian torpedo boats intercepted the *Pentcho*. Aboard the torpedo boat was a great deal of suspicion, mixed with unconcealed astonishment at the sight of a riverboat so far out to sea. The Italian captain was sure to inquire as to how they successfully navigated their way through the uncharted minefields. The bearded officer, who inspected the engines and cabins, found children playing in the filthy hold, and stated with tears in his eyes: "We are at war and endangering our lives daily, but the true heroes are you who dared to sail here with your children from Bratislava in this ship. May G-d watch over you…"[44]

The *Pentcho* was escorted to the Italian port of Stampalia whereupon the populace of Stampalia showered the refugees with wine, fruits, and vegetables. The officers gave boxes of chocolates and candies to the children aboard the *Pentcho;* then sent them on their voyage only to be rescued ten days later, again, by the Italian navy.

On the eve of Yom Kipper, the boiler exploded sending the *Pentcho* adrift and eventually wrecked on an uninhabited Italian island in the Aegean. All the passengers and crew got off the vessel before it sank a few yards from the shore.

The survivors would spend twenty months on the Italian controlled island of Rhodes in the care of a small settlement of Sephardic Jews and all continued to live as human beings under the watchful eye of the Italians. Some of the *Pentcho* refugees were eventually relocated to Tangiers; the remaining 350 were shipped to the Ferramonti internment camp in Southern Italy for the duration of the war.

When the British liberated Southern Italy in September 1943, they were astonished to find that the Italian peasants had risked their lives to protect the Ferramonti refugees from the hands of the Germans. Among the British was a team of support troops wearing British Army uniforms with the word

"Palestine" on their shoulder flashes. One of them was Reuven Franco, the Bulgarian born Revisionist agent who had given his nickname to the *Pentcho*.

With the exception of a few *Pentcho* families who opted to stay in Rhodes, the Italians were able to preserve the lives of the *Pentcho* refugees. The Nazi regime, however, took control of Rhodes, and (against Italian volition) committed most of the 2,000 indigenous Jews to Auschwitz.

Not all Alyiah Bet refugees were as fortunate as those aboard the *Pentcho*. Nevertheless, the voyage of the *Pentcho* epitomizes the risks and spirit of the Jewish resolve. As we delve further into the history of the Alyiah Bet ships, not only did several European nations sanction their own personal holocausts (pogroms) against the Jews, they acquired great wealth stripping the refugees of all their possessions, stealing their homes and businesses, divesting the Jews of any personal wealth or freedom. The destruction of the Jewish spirit, *a light in shining darkness*, however, was simply beyond their reach.

Salvador

In early December 1940, the 70-foot Bulgarian schooner *Salvador* left the port of Burgas with 327 despairing passengers. She was an old rotted out ship of Uruguayan registry, had no cabins or bunks, no compass, no weather instruments, no working engine, and only 80 lifebelts; nevertheless, the *Salvador* was successfully towed to Istanbul on her first leg of her voyage.

The only surviving picture of the *Salvador*. Some references state she was fitted with an auxiliary engine. Other sources say there was not time to complete the work. She sunk in December 1940.

After departing Istanbul, a severe storm hampered their progress. The Captain of the *Salvador* requested permission from the Turkish port authorities to return to port. His request was denied. A few hours later, in the middle of the sea with children huddled deep within her womb, a German torpedo penetrated the dilapidated hull causing the deaths of 204 passengers (including 66 children).[45] Of the 123 survivors, 63 were deported back to Bulgaria and the remaining 70 would later find their way to Palestine on the sea faring ship *Darien II*. As tragic as the sinking of the *Salvador* was, it did not discourage the Jews from fleeing Romania.

Istanbul was on the route to Palestine traveled by "illegal" refugee ships. Fearing more calamities at sea, the Turkish government (a neutral government) approached the U.S. with a plan for an orderly transportation of 300,000 Romanian Jews through Turkey to Palestine with the cooperation of the British. The U.S. Division of European Affairs, fearing the Arab reaction to a Jewish exodus to

Palestine, rejected the Turkish proposal. Furthermore, the State Department did not favor the abrogation of the British White Papers of 1939, nor would they entertain any proposal requiring the U.S. to provide transportation for escaping refugees[46] - in violation of the Jew for Oil agreement.

Ironically, over a period from 1949 to 1989, many of these 300,000 Jews who survived the death camps and pogroms of Romania, were "purchased" from the Romanian despot Nicolas Ceausescu, who in effect paroled Romanian Jews to Mossad for an average of 1,000 dollars per head.[47] Even after the war, the Mossad never gave up on their people.

Darien II

Poland had been defeated by Germany in September 1939. On November 1939, before the "Final Solution," a Mossad LeAliyah Bet envoy in Vienna secured permission from Eichmann to transport 822 Polish Jews from Vienna to Bratislava in Slovakia. They were joined by 130 refugees from Germany and 50 from Gdansk. They boarded the German riverboat *Uranus* on the Danube and headed for Yugoslavia. The refugees were subsequently transferred onto three Yugoslavian riverboats and set sail for Kladovo near the Romanian border. The refugees spent the frigid winter in Kladovo, left the riverboats and moved to a nearby community called Shavetz where another group of 200 refugees from Germany and Poland joined them.

Shavetz had a small Jewish community of 70 and a synagogue which served as a school for 20 young children.

Fortunately, 150 members of this group received their certificates and left for Palestine before the fall of Yugoslavia in April 1941. In October 1941, the remaining men of the Klavodo group were taken out into a field and shot. The Nazis took pictures of the men as they marched to the stakes where the bodies of their comrades lay before them. The women and children were put in "gas" trucks, drove through the streets Belgrade and dumped in an unknown field.[48]

The Mossad had been working all along trying to purchase a ship to rescue the Kladovo group. In May of 1940 the Mossad found and purchased a ship in Athens registered in Panama as the *Sophia S.* At once the ship was fitted with bunks, storage, latrines at bow and stern, and given a new name – the *Darien II*. The plan was that the Darien would sail to a Yugoslavian port on the Adriatic Sea and pick up the refugees from Kladovo who would come by train. The *Darien II* would eventually dock in Sulina at the mouth of the Danube waiting for the Klavodo group – a group that, much to their regret, never came.

The *Darien II*, built in Glasgow; 175 ft. in length

Before this plan could be carried out, however, the Zionist leaders in Tel-Aviv sold the ship to the British intelligence against the wishes of the Mossad. The *Darien II* sailed back to Constanza to meet up with a young Mossad agent Ruth Klüger. Ruth and her Mossad associates proceeded to commandeer the *Darien II* and her cargo of refugees and set sail for Palestine. First, they sailed to Varna, Bulgaria, then to Istanbul all the while picking up more passengers including 70 survivors from the *Salvador* and a hand full of criminals forced upon the *Darien II* by the Bulgarian police.

While in Istanbul, the Mossad had thought to return to Bulgaria and tow a barge called the *Struma* to Palestine. Unfortunately, Germany had already invaded Bulgaria and the *Darien II* had to depart. On March 19, 1941, the *Darien II* reached Haifa with 792 passengers. The ship was confiscated by the British Mandate government. The refugees were placed in the Atlit detention camp in Palestine and remained there until the end of the war. The *Darien II* was the last boat used by the Mossad during the Aliyah Bet 1939-1945 period.

Struma

U.S. and British policies did not diminish the resourcefulness of the Aliyah Bet or the Romanian Jews. Within months of the *Salvador* disaster, a private shipping agency began advertising yet another voyage to Palestine on a "luxury liner." Since the start of WWII, the Germans requisitioned all ships along the Danube to transport supplies and cattle from Romania to Germany. Finding a ship for aliyah transport was near impossible. The Germans, however, overlooked an old, abandoned cattle boat – the *Macedonia*.

The *Macedonia* measured only 148 feet long and 20 feet wide. After transporting cattle along the Danube for the past 74 years, the rotted-out hull could no longer support the weight of her cargo - of no consequence to the heartless owner determined to extract great wealth from among the wealthiest of Jewish refugees.

In December 1941, after a cursory repair and replacement of the ship engine with one of unequal worth, the owner quickly put the ship under Panamanian registry and renamed her *Struma*. Within a short period of time, 769 Jews responded favorably to the offer: 269 women (some of whom were pregnant), 103 infants or toddlers, 30 physicians, 30 lawyers, 10 engineers, a number of industrialists, merchants, craftsmen, students, and a select group of Betar leaders - none of which had neither seen or knew the true identity and condition of their rescue ship.

The *Struma* was built in 1867 as a 148 ft. iron-hulled, steam-powered schooner. She was refitted with a second-hand diesel engine.

Needless to say, the passengers were quite dismayed at the sight of their rescue ship. The *Struma* had only 100 bunks, and not a single toilet! The hull leaked, and the engine still needed serious repair. The owner was sure to inform the disgruntled passengers that an American luxury vessel lay outside the territorial waters of Romania awaiting their transfer. In haste, the *Struma* sailed from Constanza on December 12, 1941.

No sooner had they left the Romanian port, the passengers faced the harsh reality that no transport ship was awaiting them. Fear and trepidation abounded, but they had no other choice but to proceed.

Three days later they arrived in Istanbul with the ship in dire need of repair. The Turkish authorities, considering the recent catastrophe that befell the passengers of the *Salvador* graciously permitted the *Struma* to stay beyond what the transit regulations provided. In view of the unbearable conditions aboard the *Struma*, the Turkish authorities were willing to allow the passengers to disembark; however, once it was revealed that none of the passengers had entry visas to Palestine, the disembarkation was put on hold.

The Turkish Foreign Office attempted to secure visas for the *Struma* refugees; however, the British dismissed the petition claiming that as Romanians, the refugees were "enemy aliens" and, therefore, did not qualify for quotas – even though the yearly quotas established by the White Papers had yet to be filled. Having also petitioned the Romanian ambassador in Ankara to allow for the return of the *Struma*, it was concluded that since the Jews left Romania in an illegal manner, it would be impossible to readmit them. Seventy-one days later the Turkish government found themselves in a precarious position. Fortunately, the Turkish Red Cross and the JDC provided the necessary food and water to the refugees; however, the absence of sanitation facilities frustrated and demoralized the remaining 780 people on board the *Struma*.

The Turkish authorities pressured Churchill to issue visas for the 70 children aboard the Struma, a petition Churchill immediately granted. Having received news from the U.S. minister in Bucharest of the wholesale slaying of Jews whose bodies were hung and displayed on "butcher's hooks," having been granted approval from Churchill to issue visas to the children aboard the *Struma*, both High Commissioner McMichael of Palestine and the British Ambassador of Ankara were in ardent agreement: "the British government does not want these people in Palestine."[49] Colonial Secretary Lord Moyne proposed that the "Turkish authorities should be asked to send the ship back to the Black Sea ..."[50]

The Turkish authorities requested that MacMichael transfer the *Struma* refugees to another British vessel and reaffirmed their intention to keep the children on board the *Struma*. On February 23, 1942, the Turks, resigned to the fact that no transfer would take place, no goodwill, no humanitarian efforts, concession, or compromise could overcome the British intransigence, chose to take the matter into their own hands.

They too chose the non-humanitarian path disallowing the children to be transferred overland to Palestine, and proceeded to tow this overcrowded, ramshackle vessel back into the raging Black Sea, without a working engine, and abandoned her. The passengers aboard the Struma fought for their lives but were overcome by 150 Turkish police.

Early the next morning, the refugees hung over the side of the ship a banner saying: "save us." As refugees prayed for deliverance, while in the process of tending to the children, a torpedo (waking from the Turkish mainland) found its way to the beleaguered ship splitting the water-logged vessel in half. Only two survivors lived to tell of this preventable and horrific event. Upon receiving word of the fate of the *Struma*, the Turkish Prime Minister declared that "Turkey cannot be expected to serve as a refuge or a surrogate homeland for people who are unwanted everywhere else."[51]

British High Commissioner of Palestine MacMichael wanted for murder of the 779 persons on board the *Struma*

Having overruled the objection of High Commissioner McMichael, both David Stoliar (who had lost his entire family and fiancé) and Medea Salamovici were allowed into Western Palestine through "an act of clemency."

With the loss of the *Salvador* and *Struma*, all Aliyah Bet efforts came to a halt. Several private ships attempted to rescue Romanian refugees throughout 1942. Some were wrecked, yet 55 refugees survived the trip to Istanbul and took the overland route to Palestine. It was not until February 1943 that an alternate proposal was introduced to allow the exodus of Jews from the Romania butchers.

In an effort to circumvent British-American immigration policies, the Romanian government offered to release 70,000 Transnistria (Moldova) Jews for transportation costs of $50 a head, but the Roosevelt administration would only agree to the plan if the British cooperated. The Romanian government persisted, offering to transport the Jews on Romanian ships, but once again, Washington would not consider the proposal unless it received Nazi approval. Robert Alexander, a State department official, criticized any rescue proposal that would "take the burden and the curse off Hitler."[52] The British Foreign Office also reiterated that no deals with the enemy and no diversion of military resources for "Jewish causes" – an inconceivable, heartless decision that ultimately cost the lives of all 70,000 Romanian men, women, and children!!![53]

Let us not forget that the British were already spending vast amounts of military resources contending with the "illegal" Aliyah Bet ships. Why not transfer the 70,000 refugees in their Royal Navy ships, or the captured Aliyah Bet ships, or the ships used to transport captured Aliyah Bet refugees to Palestine detention camps? Treasury Secretary Morgenthau called the British message "a satanic combination of British chill and diplomatic double-talk, cold and correct, and adding up to a sentence of death."[54]

> Apart from the fact that every Jew that survived the holocaust, did so only by a miracle, millions of other Jews had miraculous opportunities to be saved but were tragically doomed by the irresponsible behavior of assimilated Jews and secular Zionist leaders. For example, secular leaders in America put enormous political pressure on the President and the State Department not to allow Holocaust refugees into the United States. They vigorously opposed religious Jews' efforts to send European Jews food, medical supplies, money and visas. Orthodox Rabbi Michael Weissmandel sent secular Jewish leaders in the U.S. detailed maps of Auschwitz and timetables of the death trains to the camp. He pleaded with these leaders to persuade Roosevelt and Churchill to bomb the camps and the railroads leading to them. His pleas fell on deaf ears. The Reform Rabbi Steven Wise was the head of the Jewish Congress when the Nazi's were willing to free 70,000 Romanian Jews for $50 apiece. He replied "… no collection of funds would seem justified." The Jewish agency (Ben-Gurion's agency) in London also denied the offer. Secular Jews pressured the U.S. State Department not to release information about the proposal to the public. Their uncompromising resolve resulted in the Romanian Jews being herded into barns hosed with gasoline, ignited, and then shot as they ran out of their infernos.[55]

It is hard to imagine that the two most powerful Christian nations in the world, knowing that since the start of WWII, of the 750,000 Jews in Romania, 400,000 had already been slaughtered in the most incomprehensible, brutal manner, could justify in their hearts the murder of innocent people - many of which were mothers and children burned and buried alive. May G-d bless those 70,000 souls who, for a brief moment, believed their salvation had arrived, and once again, perished at the hands of indifference. And what did G-d say to Abraham: *"I will bless them that bless thy seed and curse him that curseth thee."*

The Romanian Jews were not the only Jews bargained for by Nazi occupied countries. As the Romanians were slaughtering the Transnistria Jews, the Bulgarian government in early 1943 made use of Swiss diplomatic channels to inquire whether it was possible to deport non-Bulgarian Jews residing in Bulgarian occupied parts of Greece and Yugoslavia to British controlled Palestine. These Greek and Yugoslavian Jews were slated for deportation to Treblinka, but the Bulgarian government, in an attempt to save their lives, believed the British would provide safe haven for these refugees.

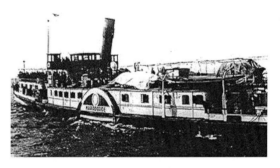

A Bulgarian riverboat transporting Greek and Yugoslavian Jews to the Treblinka death camp.

Having squandered any humanitarian effort to save 70,000 Jews from Romania, you would have thought that someone in the British government would relent and reach out to the Jews in Bulgaria; but no, the request was unceremoniously blocked by the British Foreign Minister resulting in the deportation of 3,545 adults and 592 children straight to Treblinka. Another 4,500 Jews from Greek Thrace and Eastern Macedonia were deported to Poland, and yet another 7,144 Vardar Macedonia and Pomoravlje Jews perished at Treblinka.[56] If only the Bulgarian government had utilized the services of the Aliyah Bet.

Other than Hitler and the Third Reich, what nation can willfully capitulate to the murder of 85,781 human beings? Well, the government of Great Britain sure as hell could ... and DID without hesitation or remorse! The arrogance of British aristocracy, a brood of vipers who feared not the wrath of G-d, dared to barter the lives of innocent Jews for the security of Arabian oil (another Jew for Oil trade)! Where was the U.S.? The death of these innocent victims and the unwillingness of British and American leaders to harbor the Jews prompted the Bulgarian people to reconsider the deportation of their own 50,000 Bulgarian Jews – all of which survived the holocaust.

The Bermuda Conference

In April 1943, after the entire world learned of the "Final Solution," Roosevelt and Churchill convened yet another conference to deal with the growing public outcries for the rescue of European Jewry. The Bermuda Conference was remote, almost no reporters were admitted, and no Jewish representatives were invited; obviously, considering the fact that the U.S. and Great Britain were still engaged in their own clandestine activities against the Aliyah Bet refugees.

Prior to the conference, the State Department instructed the American delegations "not to raise questions of the religious faith or race; not to make a commitment regarding shipping space for Jewish refugees; not to expect naval escorts or safe-conducts for Jewish refugees; not to pledge funds; and not to expect any changes in U.S. immigration laws."[57]

There was also to be no discussion concerning the "Final Solution,"[58] and for good reason ... Roosevelt and the British had known about Jewish extermination camps for the past year, kept it secret then, and preferred to distance themselves from the ongoing holocaust.[59] Unless otherwise forced to deal with the Jews, Roosevelt, throughout the war, refused to meet with Jewish leaders and never once mentioned the Jews in his weekly press conferences.[60] That is not to say that Roosevelt and the British endorsed, behind the scenes, the censorship of any Jewish lobbying for the right to live in their homeland. Take, for example, the Hoskins Affair.

The Hoskins Affair

To further their efforts to veto any dissention levied by Jewish operatives, Britain and the U.S. State Department embarked on a Joint Declaration that would disavow commitment to a Jewish State in Palestine and prevent freedom of expression to the Jewish minority in the United States. The Declaration proposal by Lieutenant-Colonel Harold Hoskins, backed by Roosevelt and Churchill, would have foreclosed public debate and all lobbying related to the Palestine question until the end of WWII. Furthermore, any eventual agreement would require consent of the Grand Mufti and his Arab terrorists.[61]

The Zionists groups in America united in one accord to stop this unprecedented anti-Semitic attack on freedom of speech and the G-d given right for Jews to decide where they want to live. This defeat only strengthened the resolve of British-

American leaders to prevent the escape of the Jews from European persecution and purposed to appease the Grand Mufti and the Muslim "Jew for Oil" agreement.

The Bergson Emergency Conference

On July 20, 1943, the Bergson group (individuals who sought rescue efforts of European Jews) convened a conference in New York to save the Jews of Europe. Rabbi Wise of the "Reform" Jewish Congress tried to undermine the conference and according to Nahum Goldmann (Ben-Gurion's American representative), "regarded Bergson equally as great an enemy of the Jews as Hitler."[62] Two days after the conference got under way, the chairman Max Lerner published an article in the highly regarded newspaper *PM* entitled, "What about the Jews, FDR?"

Eleanor Roosevelt cabled Lerner that if the conferees could formulate a program of rescue action, she and the American people would respond. The conferees, including Randolph Hearst, passed a series of resolutions on military and political measures, transportation admission to Palestine, treatment of Jews in Axis satellites, and temporary asylum in neutral countries: Spain, Portugal, Ireland, Sweden, Switzerland, and Turkey.

American Jews began to support and finance rescues thus operated in a political environment immensely ambivalent concerning the whole question of Jewish refugees. It was against this background that Joe Schwartz's American Jewish Joint Distribution Committee moved quietly to assist the illegal immigration of Jewish refugees to Palestine. Secretary Morgenthau and Mrs. Roosevelt managed to keep Breckinridge Lone (Assistant Secretary in the State Department, an ardent anti-Semite) in the dark about their emerging alliance with the Aliyah Bet.[63]

Bergson brought up the Emergency Committee's proposals with Eleanor Roosevelt. She passed on to FDR a copy of the recommendations of the Emergency Conference held in July, with special emphasis on the need for a rescue agency. FDR responded that nothing need be done at this time and would later "threaten that if the Bergson group's inflammatory propaganda were not curtailed immediately, he would take away the tax exemption status of all Zionist organizations in the United States."[64] **A YEAR AND A HALF** later, General Arnold of the Joint Chiefs recommended that "no reply at all should be forthcoming."[65]

The British never replied to any of the hundreds of letters and telegrams they received from the Bergson group and its supporters. The British requested that all references to the gas chambers be deleted from the Allies' Moscow Declaration of November 1943 in which Nazi atrocities against everyone but the Jews were mentioned.[66] In the end, FDR, his State Department, and the British Joint Intelligence Committee succeeded in thwarting the rescue of 4,000,000 Jews – the very Jews Bergson and Eleanor tried to rescue!!!

More "Jewish Causes"

The month after the Bermuda Conference, the Swedish government presented the Allies with a plan where it would arrange for the safe transfer of 20,000 Jewish children from Germany. Sweden offered to provide housing for the children for the duration of the war. It only asked that Britain and the U.S. share the cost of food and medicine and permit supplies to go through their naval blockade. After five months of silence, the U.S. responded that "they did not want to antagonize the Germans by limiting the rescue to Jewish children, and the plans were scrapped."[67]

Now, you have a sense of what was behind the restrictive immigration policies of the State Department. Their actions and anti-Semitic policies directly affected the outcome of the Holocaust, and yet, few questioned the criminal overtones of such policies - all sanctioned by indifference.

We should praise the men and women of the Aliyah Bet ... virtual shining lights in times of Semitic darkness and "religious" persecution.

Helsingør Sewing Club

Just for a brief moment, let us take a breath of fresh air and visit a small fishing community in Denmark – the land of HUMAN BEINGS! Here, at last, we find true Christian believers who value the life of the downtrodden and destitute ... especially the Lord's chosen people. Although the following ships were not of the Aliyah Bet, the hearts of the club members and volunteers who devised and planned the Denmark Jewish evacuation were.

As the Aliyah Bet movement continued in the Black and Mediterranean Seas, trouble was brewing in the Baltic Sea.

Most individuals in occupied Europe did not actively collaborate in the Nazi genocide; *nor did they do anything to help Jews and other victims of Nazi policies*. This most assuredly was not the case in Denmark.

One of the Danish "Helsingør Sewing Club" ships used to transfer 7,300 Jews into Sweden.

Denmark and Bulgaria were the only occupied countries that actively resisted the Nazi regime's attempts to deport its Jewish citizens. The King of Denmark strongly disapproved of anti-Semitism and refused to allow the Germans to single out Jewish citizens of Denmark for persecution. In the autumn of 1943, however, Berlin ordered the deportations of the Jewish population of Denmark, some 8,000 Jews.

Immediately, the Danish underground swung into action. The Danish fishing fleet was quickly mobilized to ferry Jews to safety across the water to Sweden. Within a two-week period, during the midnight hours, fishermen helped ferry some 7,300 Danish Jews and 680 non-Jewish family members to safety across the narrow body of water separating Denmark from Sweden. An incredible story of courage and rescue took place in Helsingør, a picturesque fishing town on the northern coast of Denmark, located only two and one-half miles across the sound from Sweden.

In defiance of human indifference, a small group of men organized what they called the "Helsingør Sewing Club."[68] Using fishing boats (including the *M0926*), speedboats, and anything else that would float, the Club made as many as ten trips to Sweden every day.

Small Danish rescue boat

The fishermen knew that if the children cried during their dangerous voyage to Sweden, they would all be in serious jeopardy. A physician in a nearby fishing village agreed to help by using sedatives to keep the children quiet during transport. In the end, only 500 Danish Jews were deported to the Nazi Theresienstadt ghetto under the watchful eye of Danish members of the International Red Cross. All but 50 of these Jews survived the war and returned to Denmark.[69]

The significance of this narrative is that the Danes proved that widespread support for Jews and resistance to Nazi policies could save lives. Instead of inciting pogroms against the Jews, instead of enacting anti-Semitic immigration policies, instead of sinking and drowning those on-board Aliyah Bet rescue ships, the Danish chose not to follow the rest of the world and did what the Lord would have done – *love thy neighbor as thyself.*

Furthermore, … when the Danish Jews returned to their homes in Denmark, they found their homes painted, businesses and gardens taken care of, and their animals alive and well; all according to the commandment "Thou shalt not steal" – a commandment the rest of Europe and religious institutions (the Vatican in particular)[70] have yet to honor.

One of the excuses the U.S. and Britain used during the war for not providing a safe-haven for the Jews is that they could not find anywhere to place them. Yes, indeed, both Denmark and Sweden attended the Evian Conference, and both agreed to the Evian Resolution. In the end, however, they chose to amend their ways and do that which was morally ethical and just. And what did G-d say to Abraham: *"I will bless them that bless thy seed and curse him that curseth thee."*

Milka

The loss of *Struma* provoked heated debates in the British Parliament. Members of both the House of Commons and the House of Lords now urged the British government to repeal the prohibition imposed on Jewish immigration to the Holy Land. Concessions were forthcoming permitting those refugees who could make their way to Istanbul would be allowed to travel overland to Syria and into Palestine.

Early in 1944, the Jewish Agency in Turkey and U.S. Ambassador Steinhardt pressured the Turkish government to supply ships for the transportation of a far greater influx of refugees. Once again, their efforts failed when Germany refused to guarantee their safety on the high seas. Meanwhile, the Mossad succeeded in arranging the purchase of several small Bulgarian ships including the *Milka* - all of which were moved to Constanza in Romania. With the Soviet troops advancing in Crimea, the Romanians gave approval to use Aliyah Bet ships to transport close to 5,000 Jewish refugees (mostly children) to Istanbul.

The Bulgarian ship *Milka* built in 1943.

The *Milka*, flying the Bulgarian flag, was the first of the Bulgarian ships to travel the torpedo laden waters of the Black Sea. On two separate trips, the *Milka* successfully transported 843 refugees to the Istanbul port. Another 1,200 (mostly children) were transported to Istanbul by the Bulgarian ships *Bella Citta* and the *Maritza* (ships bought by Americans Jewish operatives for the rescue of Romanian children).

There was one unfortunate incident that occurred during this time period – the sinking of the Turkish vessel *Mefkure* with the loss of 350 refugees. Flying a Turkish flag and a Red Cross Banner, a Russian submarine torpedoed the vessel and summarily executed the women and children in the water with machine-gun fire. Only the crew and five refugees survived.[71]

December 1944 marked the end of the Aliyah Bet movement and would not see action until after the end of the war. As fortune would have it, some 13,240 Jewish refugees passed through Turkey on their flight to Palestine with visas or at least with Turkey's tacit acquiescence.

The Cap Arcona Secret

Four days before the surrender of German forces, on December 3, 1945, a great tragedy took place on the Baltic Sea – the sinking of the *Thielbek* and the *Cap Arcona*. The narrative of these two non-Aliyah Bet ships has been kept from the public and for good reason. Ironically, the German movie version of *The Sinking of the Titanic* was filmed using the very cruise ship in this narrative – the *S.S. Cap Arcona*.

The *Cap Arcona* was a German ocean liner built in Hamburg, launched May 1927. She was 676 feet long with a service speed of 20 knots.

Contrary to the whims of some historical writers, the sinking of these ships was a "holocaust" event, whether by the hands of the Axis or Allied powers, innocent human beings ... prisoners ... were massacred. On April 14, 1945, in accordance to Hitler's order, Heinrich Himmler published his order that "no camp prisoner is to fall into enemy hands alive." Thus, the first of two notorious "death marches" commenced, destination Neustadt Bay (Baltic Sea).

Between the end of January and April of 1945 the Nazi's gassed 2,300 women at Ravensbruck. The remaining prisoners joined the mass exit of concentration camp prisoners throughout Poland and Germany. Those who fell out of ranks or broke silence were murdered along the way. On May 3, 1945, they reached their final destination.

The ship was not just any ship. Prior to the war, the massive *Cap Arcona* was known as the "Queen of the South Atlantic" carrying passengers back and forth between Germany and South America. She was the fastest in her class and fitted with every luxury. Used extensively as a German transport ship throughout the war, with her turbines no longer operable, she was towed and anchored in Neustadt Bay awaiting those who survived the "death marches."

Women in the hull of a German barge being transported from Stutthof prison camp to Neustadt Bay. Upon arrival, they were massacred where they sat with machine-gun fire by SS Officers, cadets, Hitler Youth, and townspeople from Neustadt.[72]

Of the thousands of Neuengamme, Mittelbau-Dora, and Stutthof prisoners, only 10,000 survived the death marches. At Neusadt, they were separated into two groups. The fortunate ones went with the Swedish Red Cross who had earlier negotiated the release of 500 Scandinavian women. The women were divided among two white hospital ships lying in Neustadt Bay - the *Magdalena* and *Lillie-Matthiessen*. The rest of the prisoners were transferred to the *Cap Arcona*.

The Swedish hospital ship *Lillie Matthiessen* with 225 refugees aboard, all women from Ravensbrück.

Alongside the *Cap Arcona* was the freighter *Thielbek*. Together, these mobile "concentration camps" were packed with 7,800 prisoners (5,000 men, women, and children on the *Cap Arcona* and 2,800 on the *Thielbek*).[73] Another freighter, the *S.S. Athen* was used to ferry prisoners to the *Thielbek* and *Cap Arcona*. Imprisoned within the *Athen* hull was another 2,500 prisoners. Once the ships were filled to capacity, the remaining prisoners were taken ashore and butchered with clubs, rifle butts, and shot by SS troops, cadets from the U-boat school in Neustradt, Hitler Youth, and the town people from Neustradt.

SS troops on these three ships set aside flotation devices for only themselves and the crew and smashed holes in all but a few lifeboats. The hulls of the *Cap Arcona* and *Thielbek* were filled with highly combustible fuel in anticipation of what was to follow. Captain Nobmann of the *Athen* responded: "This is the worst scandal in history."[74] On board the *Cap Arcona*, the bodies of the dead who had succumbed to typhoid fever were deposited in the bottom hold where the SS interned the Russian prisoners. "Incredibly large body lice moved over the dead bodies and onto those who were still alive."[75]

Sensing the urgency of the entire saga at Neustadt Bay, Swedish Red Cross head Hans Arnoldson, an International Red Cross witness de Blonay, and Canadian journalists Foxton and Mackenzie[76] informed the British of the thousands of concentration camp prisoners and their condition on board the *Cap Arcona* and *Thielbek*. Twenty-four hours later, early afternoon on May 3, 1945 (the day before Germany surrendered), the British responded with a Squadron of RAF Typhoon bombers heading straight for the *Cap Arcona* and *Thielbek*.

German transport ship *SS Thielbek*, built in 1940, 345 feet in length

Prisoners on board of the *Theilbek*, flying both a large white flag and a red cross flag, could see the pilots in their cockpits as they flew directly over their ship and believed their suffering had indeed come to an end.[77]

It was not to be. On the second pass, the *Cap Arcona*, *Thielbek,* and *Athen* were hit with a barrage of rockets sinking the *Thielbek* and capsizing the *Cap Arcona*. Only

350 were rescued from the *Cap Arcona*, 50 from the *Theilbek*, and fortunately, due to the heroic efforts of the captain, all the prisoners aboard the *Athen* survived the attack. The cadets along with the SS troops shot many of the survivors floundering in the frigid waters. The Typhoon bombers were also ordered to return to Neustadt Bay and strafe the prisoners in the water … none were to survive.

Those who did make it to shore, including women and children, were either bludgeoned to death by the SS or taken by the cadets and townspeople to the U-boat school, lined up in small groups, and shot. If it had not been for the arrival of the British 11th armored tanks, many more innocent victims would have perished.

It was falsely reported that the Nazi leadership planned to move to Norway and continue fighting from there and that the Germans had assembled around 500 ships in Lübeck Bay and the port of Neustadt for this purpose.[78] This was contrary to what was told to the people of Neustadt by the SS. Hamburg's SS Commander Bassewitz-Behr and Police Leader who testified at the Hamburg War Crimes Trial that the prisoners were, in fact, slated to be killed "in compliance with Himmler's orders."[79] Bassewita-Behr continued to testify that the derelict vessels were to be towed out to sea and sunk by U-boat or Luftwaffe aircraft. The 1939 Meisinger Plan for the extermination of the Shanghai Jews included such a plan.

No one came forth to identify individuals involved in the Neustadt holocaust. With the exception of the SS Camp

Commander of Neuengamme, not one of the many Germans guilty of the wholesale murder of innocent *Cap Arcona* and *Thielbek* victims have been sentenced either by British or German courts.[80] As for the Lübeck investigation into the *Cap Arcona* affair, the public prosecutor found no "clear evidence" that any wholesale killings at Neusatdt ever took place.[81] In fact, German and British governments conspired to keep this entire tragedy a secret for 100 years!

What need is there to question the motives of the parties involved. This narrative serves only to show the depth of human depravity and the moral ineptitude of governments and communities who despise righteousness and judgment; and when confronted, the spirit of indifference prevails. Then again, what need was there for the sinking of these two ships if the British forces had already arrived in Neustadt? These very forces saved 250 from the burning hulk of the *Cap Arcona*.

And let us not forget, behind the scenes, is the fact that the "Jew for Oil" agreement between Muslim oil and the British government WAS STILL IN PLACE – an agreement the historians have conspicuously ignored, an agreement the British government whole-heartedly honored until the end of 1948.

No one will ever know exactly how many died in the attacks on these ships. The victims were predominately Jewish and Eastern Europeans from twenty-four different countries. To date, neither the German nor the British government has apologized for the Neustadt Bay tragedy or have made any attempt to recognize its victims.[82] In fact, both the German and British have purposed to keep their records concealed from the public for 100 years!

Is it not the obligation of mankind to honor and remember those who died under such horrific circumstances? The Lord graciously forgives those who sin against Him; hence, any harm against our neighbor would necessitate the conciliation of forgiveness (and/or compensation) from those to whom we offend. Well-educated, arrogant elitists almost always tend to disagree, purpose to keep such "trifle" matters secret, force their will upon the less fortunate, and simply don't give a damn ... nor do they possess the spiritual capacity to understand the simple truths of sacred scripture.

The *Cap Arcona*, in 1945, with over 3,000 refugees removed within her hull.

The bodies of those slaughtered by the British, the SS and the citizens of Neustadt, were buried in a mass grave on the recreational beaches of Neustadt. As late as 1971, the bones of the *Cap Arcona* and *Thielbek* continued to wash ashore on hallowed ground. Four years after her sinking, the *Thielbek* was refloated, repaired and returned to service under the name *Reinbek*. The remains of the bodies on board were placed in 49 coffins and laid to rest in the "Cap Arcona" cemetery in Neustadt.

Many thanks to Benjamin Jacobs and Sam Pivmik who survived Hell and the sinking of the *Cap Arcona* ... and lived to tell their story in their books *The 100-Year Secret* and *Survivor*. Both books disclose the *Cap Arcona's* heart-wrenching demise, a story of unbridled hate and butchery.

It is impossible to ignore the spiritual ramifications of rogue governments who subvert justice, murder with impunity, and with a seared conscious, create their own enigmatic realm of reality.

The Zionists

It need be mentioned the Zionist role in the Aliyah Bet – a pivotal partner in Great Britain's alliance with Arab oil and the Grand Mufti. In particular are the Zionist of Aliyah *Alef* (legal immigration into Palestine) who later split with the Mossad who supported the immigration efforts of the Aliyah *Bet* (illegal immigration into Palestine) factions including the militant group called the Irgun.

A Zionist, by definition, is someone who seeks to establish a Jewish independent State, owned and operated by Jews alone. During WWII, there were secular Zionists (Alef) who sought to exclude the "poor, the down-trodden Jew, the uneducated and peasant worker." Then there were the Zionists (Bet) who purposed to open the doors to all European Jews that desired to live in their own G-d given land. The confrontation among these Zionists factions was a monumental, "behind-the-scene" cataclysm of epic proportion. Most of the information to follow has withstood the censorship of the Reformed Jewish Congress, Roosevelt's State Department, and Ben-Gurion's Jewish Agency that took control of State of Israel in 1948.

This "monumental confrontation" was, in fact, an Aliyah Bet event – one that included the entire 144 ships listed on the Aliyah Bet roster. Several organizations set out on their own to save the Jews of Europe illegally including the Revisionists, the Irgun, the New Zionists (NZO), and the Betar youth organization. During the period from 1937 to

1940, the Irgun's "illegal" immigration operation saved anywhere from nine to twenty-five thousand European Jews! An Irgun ship called the *Sakarya* brought over 2,000 refugees down the Danube route to Palestine, underscoring the fact that even with war raging, it was still possible to get Jews out of Nazi controlled territories. This contrasted sharply with the Jewish Agency, which barred anyone but their own secular "elitist" from entering Palestine. The Irgun, nevertheless, continued to support the Aliyah Bet and their quest to live in their own country.

Rabbi Stephen Wise of the American Jewish Congress condemned "the activities of independent organizations seeking to duplicate or parallel the work of the Jewish Agency." Wise ignored the fact that at that time the Jewish Agency's own activities were extremely limited and not directed toward the less fortunate, "unproductive Jew."

> "The 'Revisionists' responsible for organizing the exodus of the so-called illegals ... are solely concerned with the profit motive [the refugees paid nothing to board Aliyah Bet ships]" ... they were more than willing to take the "unsuitable – the old people, even prostitutes and criminals – certainly an element which cannot contribute to the upbuilding of a Jewish national home."
>
> Reform Rabbi Stephen Wise (1939)[83]

Yet we find Wise appealing to the British to provide certificates for the 769 occupants of the illegal ship *Struma* (mentioned earlier in this book). This vessel was filled with Europe's most eminent bankers, doctors, engineers, industrialists, and their families. Lord Moyne, the British Colonial Secretary, countered stating that if the *Struma* passengers were allowed to land in Palestine, it would have "a deplorable effect throughout the Balkans in encouraging further Jews to follow the same route" (We must, therefore, continue to honor the Jew for Oil agreement with the Arab/Muslim nations that controlled Palestine …).

When, in 1942, it was reported by the BBC and the World Jewish Congress in Geneva that 700,000 East European Jews were being gassed and exterminated, Wise authorized the release to the press. He insisted the response be kept in the lowest of keys of which the *New York Times* and the *Washington Post*, both owned by assimilated Jews, did not bother to send their own reporters to the press conference. A short article on page 10 of the *Times* reported a much smaller number of 250,000 Polish Jews.

Jewish Agency

What role did the Jewish Agency in Palestine play in the illegal immigration issue? This British conceived Agency (by British elitist - Illuminati) aligned themselves with the British Royalty, the Grand Mufti (leader of the Palestine Arabs), and Nazi war criminals Adolf Eichmann and General Kurt Becker.[84] This Agency supported the war against the Aliyah Bet and their primary leader Vladimir Jabotinsky and his militant group called the Irgun. The Agency was sure to assist the British in capturing and hanging Jewish youth who dare support Jabotinsky's General Menachem Begin and his Irgun, Aliyah Bet operatives. Jabotinsky himself had been arrested earlier for having saved 2,200 "illegal" immigrants.

"Ben-Gurion sent out special Haganah units to kidnap Irgunists. The Haganah forcibly extorted information from some of their Jewish captives and handed others over directly to the British. Ben-Gurion's men also supplied the British with the names of hundreds of other Irgun fighters and tipped off the British to the secret hiding places of the Irgun's hard-won stores of weapons … Irgun victims reported that the methods of Ben-Gurion's men were more sadistic than the techniques employed by the British in tormenting Jews."[85]

In 1947, the Bergson Group sailed from Port du Bouc near Marseilles and headed for Palestine with 700 passengers and an American crew. The *S.S. Ben Hecht* included camp survivors and Jewish refugees from Poland, Shanghai, Tunisia, France and Russia who dreamed of returning to their national home. Ben Hecht, an ardent supporter of the Bergson Group, was appalled by the labor Zionists who betrayed Irgun hide-outs (and Aliyah Bet ships) to British intelligence, and he regarded Ben-Gurion as a "stool-pigeon." Fortunately, the 700 passengers and their American crew were captured and released.

To the Bergsonites and Irgunists, Zionism meant the normalization of the Jewish People, whereas Ben-Gurion and the Jewish Agency sought to separate Jewish nationality and Jewish religion.[86] Begin threatened Ben-Gurion that if he did not set up a provisional government, the Irgun would.

Hillel Kook, alias Peter Bergson, took it upon himself to acquire military arms and a ship called the *Altalena*, after his mentor's pen-name - Jabotinsky. Both Menachem Begin and David Ben-Gurion were responsible for a squabble over the arms on the *Altalena* which led to a murderous attack on the

Irgun ship by the Haganah in June 1948 followed by a plot to assassinate Hillel Kook. Fortunately, a senior Haganah officer, Bezalel Lev, refused to go along with the plot, and Kook's life was spared.[87]

Professor Joseph Klausner, Israel's eminent historian, pronounced, "The State of Israel rests on the broken necks of twelve [Irgun men] who mounted the gallows."[88] After the State of Israel was established, Ben-Gurion avenged himself on all the Irgun and Lehi soldiers, who had fought and died saving European Jews, by denying pensions to their widows, orphans, and parents.[89] Ben-Gurion also avenged himself against the great leader, Vladimir Jabotinsky, by refusing to allow his bones to be buried in a free Eretz-Israel, as Jabotinsky had asked when dying in exile.[90]

The Jewish Immigration ship LST 138 called the *Atalena* is on fire. With the Jewish Agency approval, the Jewish Irgun ship *Atalena* approached Tel-Aviv in June 1948 carrying 930 Aliyah passengers and weapons to be used against the Grand Mufti and his band of Palestinian terrorists. It was suddenly and deliberately attacked by the Agency (at Ben-Gurion's order),[91] and sunk, killing 40 Irgun fighters. The "Mufti alliance" with Arab terrorists and their Agency operatives remains intact until this very day.[92] Ben-Gurion's Agency scrutinizes all Jews who wish to immigrate to their homeland preventing many who profess to be religious from becoming permanent citizens of Israel.

History credits the Jewish Agency and Ben-Gurion, the very agency that supported the blockade of Aliyah Bet Jews and rescue ships into Palestine, with negotiating the departure of the British from Palestine when, in fact, **the departure was due to the efforts of Jabotinsky and Menachem Begin – the leader of the Irgun!!!**[93]

> "If you were interested in the establishment of an Israeli Nation, you were involved with the right people. It was the Irgun that made the English quit Palestine. They did it by raising so much hell that we [and the Jewish Agency] had to put eighty thousand soldiers into Palestine to cope with the situation. The military costs were too high for our economy. And it was the Irgun that ran them up."[94]
>
> Winston Churchill

The American Zionists and those of the Jewish Agency were "secular" Jews who chose to abandon thousands of religious European Jews who perished in the Holocaust. The American screen-writer Ben Hecht, quoted throughout this book, supported the Aliyah Bet – the rescue of the European Jew. He authored the book *Perfidy* detailing the court records of Malchiel Greenwald vs. the Jewish Agency agent Adolf Kastner. Having overcome the death threats of those exposed in the court proceedings, having outlasted the will of the powers to be, the wife of Ben Hecht succeeded in re-publishing her husband's book in 1961.[95]

> After writing seven installments on the Kastner case. Dr. Keren flew to Germany. His intention was to interview [Kastner associate] Kurt Becher [a Nazi who was personally responsible for the death of thousands of Jews]. A few days after his arrival in Germany, journalist Keren was found dead in a German hotel. The diagnosis was "heart attack."[96]

It was an absolute miracle that any Jewish refugee survived the anti-Semitism of the American and Palestinian Zionists. The secular Zionists saved only their own, like-minded elitist. Contrary to what is written in our history books, if it had not been for the Irgun and those organizations that supported the Aliyah Bet, there may well be no Israel today. And what did G-d say to Abraham, "blessed are those who bless His children," including the poor, and the downtrodden.

> The word "Holocaust" is a biblical term for "burnt sacrifice." Why refer to genocide as "a sacrifice"? Because the Illuminati bankers deliberately sacrificed European Jews to create the State of Israel, the capital of the Rothschild's occult New World.

Prior to the death of SS Officer Adolf Eichmann (June 1, 1962), he detailed the Jewish Agency's role in helping the Nazis throughout WWII. His remarks confirm those who escaped the extermination of the 800,000 Hungarian Jews. They jumped off the "Hungarian" trains headed to Auschwitz and lived to expose the atrocities of those who sent them there – Ben-Gurion, Adolf Kastner and the Jewish Agency!!![97]

> "In my own time, governments have taken the place of people. They have also taken the place of God. Governments speak for people, dream for them, and determine, absurdly, their lives and deaths ..."
>
> The opening sentence of Ben Hecht's book *Perfidy*

And what did HaShem say?

Hannah Senesh

Hannah was born in Budapest in July 1921 and executed by a Hungarian firing squad in November 1944. As a young poet, Hannah migrated to Palestine and volunteered for a British underground operation to rescue Jews from Hungary and the Balkans. Hannah was unaware that Ben-Gurion worked for the British, was later captured by the Hungarian Police, tortured for several months then executed. The Zionist representative for the Jewish Agency (Adolf Kastner) in Hungary, having knowledge of Hannah's mission to save the Hungarian Jews, and having the authority to secure her release, made no effort to intervein. She faced her firing squad without a cover over her head and was allowed to read the following epitaph she penned the day of her execution. She was shot after the words "I lost."

> One-two-three-eight feet long
> Two strides across, the rest is dark ...
> Life is a fleeting question mark
> One-two-three ... maybe another week,
> Or the next month may still find me here,
> But death, I feel is very near,
> I could have been 23 next July
> I gambled on what mattered most, and the dice
> were cast. I lost.

Hannah's mother confronted Adolf Kastner after the war and asked why the Jewish Agency tortured and murdered her daughter. Kastner's replay was that Hannah interfered with the Jewish Agency and their association with the Hungarian Jews. If Hannah had succeeded, she may well have saved the 800,000 Hungarian Jews Ben-Gurion and Kastner farmed off to Adolf Eichmann and murdered in Auschwitz.

Displaced Persons

During the first three months that followed the defeat of Germany in May 1945, a time of crisis for American and British forces who oversaw the repatriation of prisoners, some four million Germans were sent home leaving behind 150,000 Jews still confined to concentration camps (24,000 of which were children under the age of 14).[98] From their barbed-wire compounds, Jewish displaced persons (DP's) dressed in ragtag clothing, including SS uniforms, observed a population of Germans who appeared increasingly well fed and well dressed. Of the 2,000 calories per day rationing given to the Jewish refugees, 1,250 consisted of "black, wet and extremely unappetizing bread."[99]

"Liberated" refugees eat among corpses at Bergen-Belsen Camp

Refugees at the Allach camp died in large numbers after being fed pork fat and coffee.[100] Fourteen thousand Bergen-Belsen refugees, on a diet of cabbage, perished within days when their stomachs burst open.[101] Meanwhile, the Jews seeking refuge from European post-war pogroms in Poland, Czechoslovakia, Lithuania, Austria, and Romania grew to 250,000 by the end of 1947. Thousands of Jews either dying in DP camps or fleeing from post-war pogroms throughout Europe - all taking place throughout the Nuremberg Trials! These Jews simply wanted their homes and land back.

The Joint Distribution Committee, which had since 1914 raised and spent millions of dollars to provide food and material relief for impoverished, suffering Jews in Europe and the Middle East, was nowhere to be seen ... because the Army "let only essential personnel into Germany." Voluntary agencies that might have helped with the displaced Jews were kept out of the country for fear they might get in the Army's way.

> We were hoping that some Jewish doctors in the United States would close their private practices for a little while and come to help us, if only for a month. To our great disappointment, none came."[102]

Neither the American nor the British military nor the United Nations Relief and Rehabilitation Authority (UNRRA) acknowledged that Jewish suffering and loss had been unique and that they required, as such, special assistance, enhanced rations, medical care, and Yiddish-speaking advisers.[103]

POW's were guaranteed by the Geneva Convention to get food, clothing, and medical care equal to that of their captors. The Jewish prisoners under the care of the U.S. and Great Britain, however, were confined to dilapidated Nazi concentration camps months after liberation without the required Geneva accommodations or assistance from any social service agencies (including the Red Cross). By contrast, Nazi POW's in Europe and America were granted all the amenities of most American families – none of which were without food, clothing, and medical care.

General Eisenhower issued orders to separate the Jews according to the country they had originated. This only added to the anti-Semitism, beatings, and killings within the DP camps, many of which were staffed by German and Hungarian guards - some of which were the very Nazi taskmasters that previously operated the death camps.[104] This all took place under the watchful eye of the American and British leadership.

CBS radio commentator Edward Murrow, who had moved east into Germany with General Patton and the Third Army, toured Buchenwald the day after it was liberated. In his searing commentary and his interviews with Buchenwald survivors, Murrow identified Englishmen, Frenchmen, Czechoslovakians, German Communists, professors from Poland, doctors from Vienna, men from all of Europe, but … no mention whatsoever of suffering Jews.

Dachau and its satellite camps were liberated on April 29. *Time* magazine published a first-hand report on May 7 reporting "several hundred Russian, French, Yugoslavs, Italians, and Poles were frantically hysterically happy … here were the men of all nations whom Hitler picked out as prime opponents of Nazism"[105] … but of the sixty-eight thousand main and satellite inmates, no mention of the twenty-two thousand Jewish inmates in the *Times* report.

On July 30, 1945, *Life* magazine reported that in the "American and British zones there were some 6,700,000 displaced persons. Of these, 4,000,000 (mostly German POWs) had returned home by July 12 leaving 2,700,000 Russian, French, Belgian, Dutch, Poles, and Italians under the care of Allied armies and the UNRRA" ... but, no mention of the thousands of Jews languishing in SS concentration camps without food, clothing, or Red Cross assistance.

The U.S. Office of War Information release footage of the camps taken by the Signal Corps and commercial newsreel companies. The victims identified in the newsreels include captured Yanks, Poles, Greeks, Russians, and "non-Germans" ... but no mention whatsoever of Jews.[106]

The Jewish DP's remained confined in these camps because no one wanted them. The *Washington Post* would eventually address the hypocrisy of the U.S. immigration policy. "We have exhorted the British to admit a considerable number of them [Jews] into Palestine," they editorialized. "Yet we have done nothing on our own account to afford refuge to them here."[107] According to the U.S. Displaced Persons Committee's Report, "the Veterans of Foreign Wars, the American Legion, and other groups with like views presented a solid front of opposition against assisting European Jews and/or [increased] Jewish immigration."[108]

In the summer of 1945, the newly elected President, Harry Truman, responding to reports that the American Army was treating Jewish DP's as brutally as the Nazis had, took notice and sent his personal envoy, Earl G. Harrison, to the Intergovernmental Committee on Refugees to inquire into the conditions of the Jews in the DP camps in the American zone in Germany. Harrison was accompanied on this mission by Dr. Joseph Schwartz of the American JDC. The Harrison Report did indeed change the way the Jewish DP's were treated and had a major effect on their future.[109]

What Harrison found out was that the Germans (Nazis) were receiving preferential treatment and the Jewish DP's were being "treated virtually as war prisoners, subjected to intimidation by non-Jewish DP's and to the confinement, uniforms, and food ration of [holocaust] prisoners."[110] The Red Cross was strictly forbidden to assist the Jewish DP's by order of Eisenhower and Patton.

President Truman wrote to General Eisenhower reminding him that his officers had been "directed to requisition billeting facilities from the German civilian population for the benefit of displaced persons"[111] – something they had neglected to do. May I ask, … did any of these American and British Generals advocate transporting the Jewish DP's back to their own homeland? … NO!!! Indeed, it was contrary to the Jew for Oil agreement and their alignment with the Grand Mufti.

Eisenhower did alter course and provided the very support Truman requested. He even assisted the Mossad agent Ruth Aliav-Klieger in dispatching nearly 4,000 illegal Jewish refugees to Palestine aboard two U.S. Army troopships; however, British protests put an end to further U.S. shipping of Jews.[112]

Backed by the United Nations Relief and Rehabilitation Authority, Colonel Epes in charge of the DP camps at Hart and Haag in Austria refused to obey Truman. Once again, the media brought the affair to the attention of General Mark Clark, who was in charge of the American zone in Austria. He publicly reprimanded Colonel Epes: "I don't give a damn whether or not you are interested in or in sympathy with my orders on Jews, you will obey them."[113] Soon after, Epes took over hotels in the resort town of Bad Gasten to provide rooms for the Jewish DP's.

General George Patton also voiced his "outspoken opposition to the official policy of denazification"[114] – a program designed to replace anti-Semitic and racist Nazi theories with democratic ideals and government in Germany. He wrote to his wife that "the Germans are the only decent people left in Europe."[115] President Truman sent food, clothing, medical assistance to Europe specifically for the Jews. Patton, however, gave the entire relief package to 4.5 million SS and German DP's!

When Eisenhower responded to the Harrison Report by ordering his subordinates, including Patton, to make certain reforms, Patton was loath to comply. He saw to it that the Jewish DP's were ruled with an iron hand, and many of the horrendous conditions described in the Harrison Report were at their worst in the facilities under Patton. In his diary, Patton wrote that "Harrison and his ilk believe that the DP is a human being, which he is not, ***and this applies particularly to the Jews, who are lower than animals!***"[116] The very idea of trying leading Nazis for [holocaust] war crimes offended Patton: "It is not cricket and is Semitic."[117]

Patton viewed WWII as a battle between good and evil. The only thing that mattered to Patton was victory and pompous accolades, of which, no doubt he merited. Men of G-d (Generals included) should, however, possess the moral intuition to distinguish between the wicked and the down-trodden – something Patton lacked or simply chose to ignore. Patton's anti-Semitic comments echoed the words of the German reformer Martin Luther who repeatedly demonized the Jew referring to them as "vermin and animals" – words that profoundly influenced Hitler and the German people.[118]

> "... the Jews are a base, whoring people, that is, no people of G-d, and their boast of lineage, circumcision, and law must be accounted as filth ... their synagogue is a defiled bride, yes, an incorrigible whore and an evil slut ... their synagogues and schools should be set on fire, their prayer books destroyed, [Kristallnacht] rabbis forbidden to preach, homes razed, and property and money confiscated [Nuremberg Laws] ... shown no mercy or kindness, no legal protection ... these poisonous envenomed worms should be drafted into forced labor [concentration camps] or expelled for all time ... we are at fault in not slaying them [pogroms and the holocaust]."
>
> Martin Luther
> *On the Jews and Their Lies*, 1543

The character of Martin Luther is not in question here. It is the vile verbiage that came forth from his mouth that betrayed him and the German people (and all of Europe for that matter), for literally every *articulate curse* he espoused against the Jew was embraced in its entirety by Hitler and the Third Reich providing the impetus for the many Christian pogroms throughout Europe. Regarding Luther's treatise, _On the Jews and Their Lies_, the German philosopher Karl Jaspers wrote: "There you already have the whole Nazi program."[119] And what did G-d say to Abraham: _"I will bless them that bless thy seed [Israel]... and curse him that curseth thee."_

No doubt Patton was a great General and leader. So too, was King Nebuchadnezzar of Babylon, the Assyrian General Sennacherib, and Titus of Roman, all of whom succumbed to arrogance and unmitigated hatred of the Jews; and all perished at the hand of G-d. Patton was relieved of his responsibilities and soon afterwards died as the result of injuries sustained in a "suspicious" automobile accident.

Soon after Patton's death, Eisenhower reported having raised the food portions; clothing and shoes were finally made available to Jewish DP's and medical attention. To protect the Jews from German indifference, Eisenhower ordered the separating of Jewish DP's from the rest of the DP population. Special centers were established for "those Jews who are without nationality or those Soviet citizens who did not desire to return to their country of origin."[120]

* * *

As early as October 1945, the first Zionists (Bet) from Palestine began arriving in Eastern Europe. Jews lived in Palestine for thousands of years before great numbers of them had fled successive pogrom massacres by both Christians and Muslims. These Zionists (Bet) were committed to re-creating a homeland in Palestine for the homeless and displaced Jews, and once again called upon the Mossad and their rescue fleet of Aliyah Bet ships. Their organized exodus from Eastern Europe became known as the *Bricha* (Hebrew for "flight").

As you study the following Bricha Section, bear in mind that the *Cap Arcona* Jews, the Jews Roosevelt and the State Department mustered for Hitler, the Jews the Arab terrorists (armed by the British) murdered in Palestine throughout the war, the Alyiah Bet men, women and children the British murdered and those the British Royal Navy abandoned at sea after taking their food, water, and fuel, the thousands of post-war Jews massacred by European nations who stole their land and homes, and those the nations abandoned and who perished in the DP camps were not counted among the "six million" recorded in history books. And what did the Lord say will become of these Edomite nations[121] that contended with his children (historically over 600 million Jews), the very nations that contend with Israel today(?) ...

Approach, O nations, and listen, for the Lord is angry at all the nations ... He shall measure the land of Edom with a line of chaos and with weights of emptiness. The land shall be called, "No kingdom is there," its nobles and all its lords shall be NOTHING.

(Isaiah Chapter 34)

Bricha
(1945 – 1948)

After the end of WWII, preparation for the Nuremberg trials got underway. Conspicuously absent from the tribunal of Nuremberg judges was a representative from what was to become the State of Israel. Jews remained confined in concentration camps or found themselves once again victims of European and Arab post-war pogroms. During the first nine months of 1945, 351 Polish Jews were "murdered on trains or thrown out of running trains by the Polish population."[122] In Cracow, Poland and Slovakia (August 1945) many Jews were murdered and their property destroyed.

> In the summer of 1946, there was a terrible pogrom, shocking in its cruelty, in the city of Kielce. It took place in broad daylight, under the gaze of the local police (and some say with their participation). Jews who had managed to survive the German occupation now found their death in the city of Kielce and its environs, at the hands of Polish murderers. More than 42 Jews were killed; the government was too weak to prevent the catastrophe. The axe blows in the heads of the Kielce victims reverberated throughout Poland; Jews who had hoped to return and to rebuild their lives in that country experienced a rude awakening. After Kielce, there was no longer any hope for Polish Jewry except in flight.[123]

The British revised their White Paper edict of 1939 adding even more restrictions to Jewish immigration, including Arab control of Jewish entry quotas. British efforts to block the migration led to violent resistance by the Zionist (Bet) underground. Illegal immigrants detained by the British Government were interned in deplorable camps on Cyprus. Those interned included a large number of children and orphans who lived as prisoners for several years.

The Cyprus compounds were surrounded by barbed wire and armed guards. There was no running water, no sanitary facilities, and no Barracks. The refugees were confined to tents and subjected to soaring temperatures. Captain Rudolph Patzert, a U.S. commander of one of the "illegal" ships, was captured by the British and spent two years in a Cyprus internment camp. According to Captain Patzert, the Nazi POW's had better accommodations than the Jewish refugees, were treated differently, and repatriated when the war ended. The Jews, however, remained interned until February 1949 when the last group of detainees left for what had become the State of Israel.[124]

Several Jewish organizations (including Revisionists) came together to facilitate this new stage of Ha'apala called the *Bricha*. This was a Mossad run operation designed to find homes for the thousands of Jewish DP's languishing in refugee camps in occupied Germany and those fleeing the European post-war pogroms.

The Hagana Ship *Theodor Hertzl* in Haifa Harbor

The Jewish Agency in Palestine set up an organization called *Mossad Le'Aliyah Bet* to coordinate the attempts to bring refugees into the country. The Bricha quickly multiplied into a number of loosely structured organizations (i.e. the Polish, Czechoslovak, and Austrian Bricha) that cooperated increasingly with one another to protect Jewish refugees and to open roads to Palestine. Bricha finances came from a variety of relief sources; however, it was primarily the support of American Jewish organizations and the JDC that kept the entire operation afloat.

Mossad reached the peak of its activity in this stage. In three years, 1945-1948, they bought and equipped 64 ships that sailed 140 times from ports in France, Italy, Yugoslavia, Greece, Bulgaria, and Romania.[125] About 70,000 holocaust survivors sailed to Israel, most were caught and deported to Cyprus, a few managed to enter without being caught.

> Behind the Exodus scene was an ongoing pogrom against Israel by [British supported] Palestinian Arabs. Between November 1947 and May 1948, more than 4,000 Jewish soldiers and 2,000 Jewish civilians had been killed, nearly 1 per cent of the total Jewish population.[126] It was a British mandate (a Jew for Oil mandate) for Jews in Israel not to possess weapons!

Fede

The charter of the *Fede* in May 1946 and the Haganah double agent who chartered the vessel exemplified the true resourcefulness of Jewish intelligence. The success of the *Fede* quickened the Aliyah Bet resolve and for the first time openly exposed to the world the clandestine activities perpetuated upon the European Jews throughout WWII by the British Royal Navy.

This narrative involves a delightful character named Yehuda Arazi, referred to by the British as the "Scarlet Pimpernel." Working as a double agent for the Haganah, Arazi, serving in the British police force, successfully penetrated their intelligence network. He smuggled British arms to the Haganah and helped Jews in Poland, the Balkans, and North Africa to escape to Palestine. He would later create a "phantom army unit," forged requisition papers, and set up a smuggling operation in Milan, Italy.[127]

Using British demobilized Jewish Brigade personnel, Arai set up military police (MP) signboards, guard posts, and a facility to produce all the documents he needed to satisfy the British that this was a legitimate army operation. Issuing phony papers, Arazi requisitioned a fleet of new vehicles. These vehicles not only transported refugees up and down the coast of Italy to awaiting rescue ships their drivers also used forged orders for clothing and provisions to provide for those sailing to Palestine. The British were increasingly furious at their inability to stop the operation.

In late 1945, Arazi designed and constructed several small vessels (schooners) that could accommodate 80 refugees. During the next two years he succeeded in sending over twenty ships with 11,415 immigrants to Palestine. In the spring of 1946, Arazi arranged yet another daring and eventful aliyah voyage for the Mossad – one that would capture the attention of the world.

Arazi chartered a large vessel, the *Fede*, and obtained an Italian license to carry a cargo of salt from the Italian Riviera to the island of Sardinia. Four months earlier, the *Fede* had transported 1,024 Polish refugees to Palestine undetected. Having gained the sympathy of the port authority police, several trucks of Polish refugees were allowed to board the

Fede. Unfortunately, the British found out prior to their departure and prevented the *Fede* from leaving the port. Arazi went public telling a variety of news organizations that a thousand Holocaust survivors were jammed onto a leaky tub, which was under siege by tanks, guns, and ships of the British navy. Reporters descended upon the scene to cover the story as did the Italian public.

The *Fede* sailed three times (one legal and two illegal) to Palestine carrying a total of 2,846 refugees.

Azari got hold of a public-address system and made daily speeches to the crowds, telling them that all Hitler's victims wanted was to go to their homeland in Palestine. The Italian police forced the British to retreat from the docking area. The Italian prime minister, the admiral of the Italian fleet, and other notables around the world proclaimed sympathy for the hunger strikers.[128] Then, Azari announced that if the ship was not allowed to sail immediately, each day ten DP's would kill themselves on deck in full view of the crowds and journalists gathered on the dock.

The British capitulated and agreed to the immediate admission of all the 1,014 passengers without regard to the quotas in effect in Palestine. This event proved to be a turning point for the Aliyah Bet, for the first time in their rescue efforts they had the support of world media.

S.S. Smyrnie and S.S. Alba Julia

Ira Hirschmann, a U.S. War Refugee Board representative, became one of the conduits for JDC funding for the acquisition of ships to transport Jews from Romanian and Bulgarian Black Sea ports to Istanbul in route to Palestine. In mid-1946, in concert with the Jewish Agency and the Mossad, Hirschmann and Joseph Schwartz (JDC) arranged for the illegal transport of 8,000 Jewish refugees from Constantsa to Istanbul in a flotilla of small, leaky boats including the Romanian ships *Smyrnie* and the *Alba Julia*.

Romanian passenger-cargo ship *Smyrnie*

Schwartz authorized three million dollars to finance this expedition, the largest sum yet spent by the Joint on a single operation – the largest single rescue of Jewish refugees throughout the entire war. Ironically, the British intelligence officers in Turkey (in anonymity) chose to work intimately with the Mossad on this Joint mission.

Ile de Rosa

The French schooner *Ile de Rosa* was one of the few "sailing" vessels used by the Mossad to transport refugees from Italy to Palestine. A few months earlier, the British intercepted the Bricha ship *Lochit* killing two and severely beating a number of the 3,845 refugees. Despite the danger that awaited them, the crew of the *Ile de Rosa* prepared for their journey and set sail from Bacoli (north of Naples) on August 1946 with 183 refugees.

The French schooner *Ile de Rosa*.

The crew of the *Ile de Rosa* was French, one of which was lost at sea. The British paid no attention to her because she was sailing under a French flag. The *Ile de Rosa* was one (the first) of only four *Bricha* ships that successfully delivered its valuable cargos undetected.

Ulua

A few months before the end of WWII the Swedish Red Cross made desperate efforts to save Jews. Contact was established with Gestapo leaders and Himmler himself who eventually agreed to hand over to Sweden several thousand girls still languishing in concentration camps. From Auschwitz, Bergen-Belsen and other camps, trains full of women and girls suddenly began to move. To the astonishment of the women, the trains moved north – not the usual death path of the Germans. They were transferred to large ferries and much to their amazement, soon found themselves in Sweden where they were treated with great compassion by the people of the Red Cross.

Their meeting with other Jews was a traumatic experience. "They saw Jews who were well dressed, well fed, secure, crowding together at the quarantine fences to welcome them with cries of "Shalom Aleichem" (welcome), weeping bitterly at the sight of the newcomers – ill, hungry, emaciated, and in tatters."

Many of these girls had relatives who were urging strongly that they be brought to Israel as quickly as possible. It was this pressure which brought the Mossad into the picture. This would be the first attempt by the Mossad to rescue Jews from Sweden. A Mossad team was sent to America to purchase a sturdy ship. While in Florida, the agents fell in love the moment they saw the *Ulua*. She was an obsolete, small naval vessel built before WWI for the U.S. Coast Guard, survived two wars as an escort vessel, sold to a South American firm which converted the *Ulua* into a freighter carrying fruit from Central America and the Caribbean.

The *Ulua* was purchased and sailed to Marseilles, France for refitting. All partitions were ripped out below decks and all superfluous equipment was removed. The officer and crew mess rooms were dismantled to gain every possible inch of space for the 1,000 refugees. In the open space were constructed five or six tiers of long planks, dividing them into bunks about five and a half feet long and sixteen inches wide, with about eighteen inches high and aisles less than two feet wide. The kitchen was enlarged and installed with large cooking cauldrons which, using the ship's steam, could prepare food for a thousand people at a time. A dozen showers and two dozen toilets were installed. The *Ulua* was stocked with canned meat, fruit, sugar, cheese, powdered milk, and eggs. Several fuel tanks were added to the ship for the long voyage.

Ulua preparing for the Mossad voyage in 1946 to Palestine from Sweden

The crew of the *Ulua* consisted of non-Mossad members, three Palyam seaman (members of a special Jewish unit called the *Palmach*) who were to oversee the refugees, and one Mossad in charge of the entire operation. The captain of the *Ulua* was a veteran captain living in exile in Marseilles. Captain Pedro Lopez and his crew of four Spaniards manned the deck and engine-room.

On January 1, 1947, the *Ulua* departed Marseilles, sailed through Gibraltar and headed toward Denmark. The British, having full knowledge of the Mossad ship and its mission, had the Danish Royal Navy confine the ship in Copenhagen. The Commandant of the Port of Copenhagen, a Jewish sympathizer did not comply. He realized that many of the Swedish refugees the *Ulua* was attempting to deliver to

Palestine were the very refugees he helped rescue from Denmark in 1943. The Commandant resupplied the *Ulua* with fuel and supplies and sent her on her way.

The *Ulua* entered the Trelleborg harbor (Sweden) openly and legally with the collective visas permitting all the refugees from Sweden to enter Cuba (the pre-supposed destination). The refugees boarded the ship, most of which were young teenage girls, and settled into their bunks without issue. A pilot of the Swedish Royal Navy boarded the ship and guided the *Ulua* through the Straits of Skagerrak and Kattegat.

There were several able minded cooks among the refugees who prepared a variety of tasty hot meals throughout the voyage. They traveled to Le Havre, France, then across the Bay of Biscay, through the Strait of Gibraltar to Algiers, Philippeville, Sousse, Tunisia, then to Metaponto and Gallipoli, Italy. They picked up 850 passengers in Metaponto including 50 homeless children who had been waiting for a ship to Palestine.

Four British destroyers were waiting for the *Ulua* once they departed Gallipoli. Two submarine chasers from Haifa joined the flotilla. The captain of the British destroyer was sure to communicate to the *Ulua* (renamed *Haim Arlosoroff* by the Mossad) that under the Mandatory Government, they were breaking the law and are entering the borders of Palestine illegally – the Jewish, not the British, Arabic, or any other nation's homeland. From the *Ulua* came the response in English:

"Sailors of the British Navy, before you is a ship of Jewish refugees who are returning to their homeland after a long exile and after the murder of their people by Hitler and the Nazis. It is not we but you who are violating humanity's law by detaining us. It is not we but you who are in this country illegally. The Land is ours and ours she will continue to be. Our brothers are standing on shore waiting for us. No one will stop us. We shall resist you – and win."[129]

The British responded by shooting the *Ulua's* spotter in the crow's nest several times before he fell to his death upon the deck, then rammed and punctured the *Ulua's* hull. The troopers stormed the *Ulua* gassing and seriously clubbing many into submission. Before the British could get control of the pilot house, however, the *Ulua* ran aground on a reef not far from the Palestine shore where she remained firmly planted for the following two years. The 1,850 refugees were shipped to Cyprus and eventually transferred to Palestine as citizens of the new State of Israel.

Wrecked *Ulua* on Palestine reef.

Many of the refugees met their soul-mate on board the *Ulua* including the Mossad agent himself. This wonderful story can be found in Arie Eliva's book *The Voyage of the Ulua* dated 1969.

Orietta

On April 14, 1947, 2,552 refugees on board the *Guardian* were captured trying to reach Palestine. Of this number, three were killed by the British boarding party. On April 22, 769 refugees arrived on the *Galata*, followed by the *Trade Winds* on May 17 with 1,442, on May 24, another 1,457 aboard the *Orietta*, then on May 31 the arrival of 399 refugees aboard the *Anal*. The vast surplus of post-war ships strengthened the resolve of the Aliyah Bet and the quest of Zionism.

The *Orietta.*

Exodus

Among the Aliyah Bet ships during the *Bricha* was a fleet of "secret ships" that have mysteriously eluded our history books. Starting in 1946, at the request of the Mossad, a fleet of ten aging vessels purchased by Jewish Americans in the U.S. and manned by volunteers from American, Canada, and Latin America who joined the Aliyah Bet effort. They sailed their war surplus ships from America to European ports, picked up their cargos of Jewish refugees, and headed straight for Palestine. The men who crewed these ships were young, most of which had very little if any sailing experience.

More than 32,000 Jewish refugees sailed on board these American rescue ships. Of the 64 ships that sailed during the *Bricha* era of the Aliyah Bet, none became more widely known as the *Exodus* and her 4,500 refugees whose harrowing experience perpetrated by the Royal Navy captured the attention of the outside world.

The *Exodus*, formerly the *President Warfield*. Launched in 1928, she was 320 ft. in length.

Built in 1928 by the Baltimore Steam Packet Company, the *President Warfield* was launched as the new flagship for its small fleet of excursion liners plying the Chesapeake Bay between Baltimore and Norfolk. She took part in the Normandy invasion and served as a troop transport until the end of WWII. The Warfield returned to the Chesapeake Bay and sat unused in the James River for a year. After several transfers of ownership, she ended up in the hands of the Aliyah Bet … and so began her clandestine career as an "illegal" immigration ship.

Stowed aboard the *President Warfield* was canned drinking water, life jackets, army K-rations, and three million cigarettes that could be sold on the black market in Europe to help pay for operational costs. The volunteer crew of 42 assembled on the main deck, took the Haganah oath and received a Bible and sweater. All attempts by the British government to avert the *President Warfield* from reaching the French Port-de-Bouc failed. On shore, 70 trucks filled with 4,500 refugees boarded the ship, the mooring lines were cut, and *President Warfield* made its way out to sea.

The British amassed a small task force consisting of the cruiser *Ajax*, four destroyers, a frigate, and two minesweepers to confront the 4,500 refugees aboard the fleeing *President Warfield*. Finally, early in the dark hours of the morning, 23 miles off the coast of Palestine, the British illuminated the refuge vessel with their searchlights. Blue-and-white Jewish flags flew from her staffs fore and aft, and signs in English proclaimed her new name as "Haganah Ship – *Exodus 1947*."[130]

The war ships proceeded to ram the *Exodus* seven times before boarding her. The Marines made their way to the wheelhouse and clubbed to death the Second Mate, American volunteer Bill Bernstein.[131] For two hours the refugees fought with iron bars, wooden bats, bottles filled with nails and screws, cans of food, and anything else that could be wielded or thrown.

Near daybreak, frustrated with the unyielding Jews, the British used small arms fire on deck and morally wounded two Jews, one of them an orphan of 15 years of age who was shot in the face for throwing an orange.[132] In all, 146 Jews had been injured; 28 of them were hospitalized.

Upon reaching Haifa, the refugees, under duress, were dragged, beaten, and forced aboard three prison ships, confined in cages, and set sail for Cyprus. Upon arriving, the British officer in charge was ordered to divert the deportation back to Port de Bouc. Determined to make an example of the *Exodus*, and angry about her escape from the harbor at Sete, British Foreign Secretary Blevin wanted the passengers returned to France.

Upon arrival at Port-de-Bouc, only 60 infirm and elderly passengers agreed to go ashore; the others refused, and the French government announced that it would not force them. Three weeks later, hearts hardened and indifferent to the plight of these holocaust victims, the three ships set sail for the British zone in occupied Germany.

Upon arrival at Hamburg, 2,500 British troops stood ready at the harbor with tear gas and clubs. Refugees were dragged off the first two ships, but the Jews refused to leave the third ship and battled for two hours against 300 paratroopers and military police. A crowd of Germans gathered to watch the incredible scene of Jews being beaten by those who had so recently won the war against Hitler. Once overpowered and removed from the prison ships, the refugees were confined once again in the holocaust prisons of their former enemy.

Through the determination of one Jewish journalist Ruth Gruber, who witnessed the *Exodus* enter the Haifa harbor then followed the refugees to the French Port-de-Bouc, the plight of the Jewish holocaust refugees catapulted across the globe. Gruber was allowed by the British to accompany the DPs back to Germany. Aboard the prison ship *Runnymede*

Park, Gruber photographed the refugees, confined in a wire cage with barbed wire on top, defiantly raising a Union Jack flag on which they had painted a swastika.

Ruth Gruber revealed to the world the British "Jew for Oil" atrocities.

Members of the United Nations Special Committee on Palestine (UNSCOP) who also witnessed the arrival of the *Exodus* at Haifa port, hailed the plight of this "holocaust" ship and its occupants to be the single most event that predisposed the creation of the Jewish State of Israel in 1948.[133] Had it not been for the journalistic efforts of Ruth Gruber, their story might well have been sealed in obscurity as were all German, American, and British documents relating to the "illegal" ships whose "illegal" immigrants were covertly persecuted, killed, and abandoned throughout the war under the anti-Semantic directives of the United States and Great Britain.

> What happened to our people in this war is merely a climax to the uninterrupted persecution to which we have been subjected for centuries by almost all the Christian and Moslem peoples in the old world.[134]
>
> David Ben-Gurion
> First Prime Minister of Israel

The State of Israel

Britain relinquished her control over Palestine, and on May 14, 1948, the State of Israel was born. President Harry Truman signed the letter of recognition – despite the objections by the United States Secretary of State George Marshall, the U.S. State Department, and Great Britain (who chose not to support the United Nations resolution).

> The truth is suppressed that UN Declaration 181, November 29, 1947, gave Israel only about 18 percent of the land that the League of Nations in its 1922 Declaration of Principles set aside for a Jewish homeland. Unhappy with being given only 82 percent of what didn't belong to them, and demanding it all, six Arab nations attacked the new state of Israel with their regular armies.[135]

This same British country that supplied the Arab nations with weapons to subdue the Jews, passed laws against Jews acquiring weapons and organizing militia forces,[136] and blew up Jewish humanitarian flotillas after the Holocaust, had the audacity to condemned Israel for halting politically inspired flotillas [and weapons] to Gaza in 2010.

> When on May 31, 2010, The British government denounced as "completely unacceptable" the way that the Israelis landed troops on the Turkish flotilla to Gaza, we did not know that its predecessor had done much the same, actually blowing up one ship and damaging two more vessels of a genuinely humanitarian flotilla that was trying to bring Jewish survivors of the Nazi death camps to their forefather's ancient homeland.[137] All was accomplished through MI6 (the British Secret Intelligence Service) with primary consideration that "no proof could ever be established between positive action against the traffic [Aliyah Bet ships] and His Majesty's Government [HMG]," thus the code name Project Embarrassment.[138]

The establishment of the State of Israel effectively ended the Ha'apala of which more than 108,500 refugees found their way to Palestine in Aliyah Bet ships.[139] Those lost at sea include 1,600 who perished in private and Aliyah Bet ships attempting to reach the shores of Palestine and many more who perished on board the German ships *Cap Arcona* and *Thielbek*.

Yet, if it had not been for the Jews smuggled into Palestine between 1938 and 1948, Israel could not have won its War of Independence. At the time the nation was born, one out of every three Israelis was an illegal smuggled into the country by nine men and a beautiful young redhead named Ruth Klüger. This tiny group, the Mossad, had successfully operated the largest rescue movement in recorded history.

Honor and Indifference

Whatever became of Ho Feng-Shan and Chine Sugihara? Because of their courage and moral convictions, both Ho and Chine were awarded the honorable title of "Righteous among the Nations" by the Israeli organization Yad Vashem.[140] As for Gustav Schröder, the German Captain of the *St. Louis*, he was tried for war crimes and found guilty ... of saving the lives of 700 Jews, was awarded the Order of Merit by the Federal Republic of Germany and lived what appeared to be a pauper's life. Israel reciprocated by awarding Schröder the distinguished "Righteous among the Nations" – an award most precious in the eyes of man and G-d. In 2000, the German city of Hamburg named a street in honor of Schröder and unveiled a detailed plaque at the landing stages.[141]

Happy is the people whose G-d is the Lord, the nation
He has chosen for His own inheritance.

King David, Psalm 33:12

One thing Breckinridge Long, the U.S. Assistant Secretary of State for European Affairs (who exercised complete power over granting visas), Roosevelt, U.S. Secretary of State George Marshall, Patton, Churchill, the British Foreign Secretary Blevin, the British High Commissioner of Palestine MacMichael, the Grand Mufti, Rabbi Wise, Ben-Gurion, and Hitler all had in common – they ignored the Word of G-d, persecuted the Lord's chosen, and frankly "didn't give a damn" … and, of course, we know what G-d said to Abraham.

But for Your sake __we__ are killed all day; __we__ are considered as
sheep for the slaughter.
Psalm 44:23

Such are they who seek power, glory, and despise wisdom. Ultimately, their arrogance and unsympathetic hatred of the Jews could not and did not amend the Will of the very G-d they fought.

It is well documented that many, but not all, of the Jewish oppressors stood trial for crimes against humanity. Aside from those the U.S., Great Britain, and Russia spirited away into anonymity, the indifference of the U.S., Great Britain, and the Jewish Agency against the Aliyah Bet refugees has never been formerly addressed and perhaps never will be.

Not only did these governments engage in the clandestine killing and oppression of the Lord's anointed, having denied them safe-haven in their own country, they purposely submitted to the holocaust with their anti-Semitic hatred.

It is inconceivable that a people, few in number, could bear such hatred among the nations of this world. WWII was far more than an imperialist showcase of aggression; it was an unprecedented, well-orchestrated pogrom of supernatural dimension against the Lord's anointed. Consider the words of Hitler in his last stated address ... **His** words, not the words of Christian journalists and historians.

> "It is true we are barbarians. It is an honorable title to us. I am freeing humanity from a false vision called conscience and morality. The Jews have inflicted two wounds on mankind – circumcision on its body and conscious on its soul. The war for world domination will be fought entirely between us, the Germans, and the Jews. All else is façade."
>
> Hitler

Now consider the words of 48 prophets recorded some 2,500 years ago about Germany and the descendants of Haman – Esau (Edom). Also written in the Hebrew Gemara of 500BC is a prophecy involving 300 Barbaric tribes that would unite (Germany) in the future and purpose to annihilate the Lord's anointed. Queen Esther, in the Book of Esther, prophesied the very date and number of Haman's descendants (the ten Christian Edomites that were hung at the Nuremberg trials) that would be convicted as war criminals in 1946.

So too did the Sages state in the *Talmud* that the country Esther prophesied about would be derived from 300 blonde hair, blue eyed barbarian tribes, bearing the name of "Germania" (the very name Hitler intended to re-name

Germany). Julius Streicher, the last descendant of Haman hung, confirmed the totality of the Third Reich with his last words: "Purimfest 1946!"

"Julius Streicher, who hanged himself with his pen, may well have been the most despised man of WWII on either side." Julius was the key figure in the Nazi propaganda machine.

Blaine Taylor
Warfare History Network

How often do we find in the *Torah* G-d sending his prophets to Israel warning them against assimilating among the Gentiles?[142] They did not listen and were destroyed. So too, did Esther and the Sages prophetically warn the European Jew against assimilating among the German people of which some 1,400 synagogues were ultimately destroyed the night of Kristallnacht ... all of which were Reform Jewish synagogues!

The day is coming, according to King David, when the nations of the world, sailing upon their "ships of Tarshish," will come against Israel in the war of Gog and Magog. Could it be that these "enemy aliens" that dare to destroy His anointed will once again include the war ships of the Royal Navy?

It has been written that *a woman with a blood issue* reached out and grabbed the ***tzitzit*** of a Jew and was cured (Matthew 9:20-22). In the end times, when *the Gentiles shall come from the ends of the earth and say: Our fathers inherited utter delusions, things that are futile and worthless*[143] ... *these nations of the world will* (once again) *seek the **tzitzit** of every Jew* (Zechariah 8:16-23) to teach them about the *G-d of Israel* and His *Torah*. May the Lord bless the Aliyah Bet, the poor and down-trodden Jew, and the righteous Gentiles who purposed to make this salvation event possible for ***all*** of mankind!

President Truman found himself in a predicament. His Generals did not obey him. The United Nations did not respond to the call. Roosevelt's War Refuge Board abandoned the Jews languishing in the German concentration camps, and pogroms against the Jew were, once again, in full swing. Truman prayed to G-d for mercy and G-d answered Truman with a *name* – the very name G-d chose to rescue the Jews of Europe ... "Eleanor Roosevelt"! It was this gentle soul, the only one, that visited the down-trodden Jews in their camps, spoke to the leaders of the world on their behalf, and won the approval of the nations who brought the homeless Jews back to their homeland.

That, my friend, is the power of a G-d fearing woman!

Reflection

Concerning the holocaust ... my perspective, subject to nebulous inclination, is what motivates, or should I say, captivates my thoughts. Nations, policies, Generals, battles, military secrets, weapons of war, casualties are mere subtleties of my youthful imagination, intangible though they may be, yet emblematic of my very person.

Our words and deeds can and do reveal the true condition of our heart. Knowledge, the quintessence of thought and deed, void of spiritual understanding can impede our acquisition of wisdom from which our soul derives its strength. Such knowledge began nibbling at my soul back in 1967 as I sat, with my father, listening to the PBS commentator broadcast the daily events of the Arabic/Israeli 6-Day war.

My father was not an affectionate individual, nor one to impart words of wisdom, and never divulged his innermost thoughts (at least not to me). Just prior to his death, however, my father was not without a blessing for his eldest son. As fate would have it, we found ourselves summoned once again by the PBS commentator as he interviewed a host of holocaust survivors. A few minutes into the broadcast, my father slid to the side of his chair and gently spoke these words to me: "Be kind and bless the Jews, for they have suffered greatly." Without a doubt, the call of death can indeed quicken the spirit.

The words of my father, the very last words he ever spoke to me, planted a seed deep within my heart. The Lord was sure to provide a Gardner to nurture His seed – my dear wife

Peggy, who would introduce me to Maimonides, Rashi, the *Torah*, and the Sages. Having earlier succumbed to indifference, the seed of providence quickened my spirit to the plight of the Jews throughout WWII.

Don't ask. ... I can only tell you it all started with my reading John Bierman's book *Odyssey* and constructing a model of the *Pentcho*. Next was the *Darien II*, followed by the *Salvador*, then the *Struma*, quickened by the cruise ship *Cap Arcona* and freighter *Thielbek*, then the cruise ships *Conte Verde* and *S.S. St. Louis*, the *Milka,* the *Orietta,* the *Ile de la Rosa*, the *Exodus*, a host of Danish rescue vessels, and von Luckner's *Seeadler*. My wife can attest to the fact that the "seed of passion" bequeathed to me by my father, once nurtured, has blossomed.

The Lord's ever-growing model collection of *Alyiah Bet* and holocaust ships has brought blessing, strength, and spiritual understanding into my heart. These ships and their stories paint an entirely different picture of what took place behind the scenes of valor, strategy, and victory – a spiritual battle of the highest order. Although the cast of Jewish refugees have all but perished, their saga of eternal memories and needful sorrow remain.

The nations that betrayed the Jews 70+ years ago still cling to their territorial "pogrom" against the Jews. We find the spirit of indifference in one accord within the Christian-Muslim alliance, both determined to forsake the G-d of Israel and His Prophets of old and do so with impunity. Need it be said that the Holy Bible and Koran both state the land of Canaan was promised to Abraham and his seed, Israel. Furthermore, the *Torah* informs us that Joshua conquered the seven heathen nations of Canaan with the exception of three territories. The Lord informed Joshua that these territories would be a thorn unto Israel until the arrival of the Messiah.

> Recall that Moses said to his people, 'O my people, remember G-d's blessings upon you: He appointed prophets from among you, made you kings, and granted you what He never granted any other people. O my people, enter the holy land that G-d has decreed for you, and do not rebel, lest you become losers."
>
> From the Koran: Sura 5:20-21

Joshua's disobedience greatly displeased the Lord,[144] for He knew the peoples of these territories would continue to rebel against His authority. Those three territories include the Gaza strip, the West Bank, and the Golan Heights – the very territories America, Great Britain, and the United Nations, with unyielding determination, demand of Israel to relinquish. The Prophet Joel was quite clear as to what will become of the nations of Edom (Christianity) and Ishmael (Islam) at the *end of days* who will divide up and give away the land of Israel.

Indifference is not a disease nor is it genetically manifested. Its presence, however, pre-disposes the thoughts of man. Indifference towards the *Torah* of G-d is one thing; indifference towards G-d's Holy people is another matter altogether. Jews have endured the likes of Nebuchadnezzar, Sennacherib, Haman, Herod, Titus, Christian and Muslim Crusades, the Spanish, Portuguese, and Roman Inquisitions, decades of anti-Semitic pogroms, the holocaust, four Arabian wars, Palestinian terrorists, Christian missionaries, and Great Britain. What Gentile nation has ever endured such hatred and persecution? Is it any wonder G-d calls these Guardians of the *Torah* "the blessed among nations?" It is not the Holocaust, however, that is in question here; but instead, man's unwillingness to sanctify the *Name* of the G-d of Israel and keep His Commandments.[145]

It was G-d who led the Jews to Aliyah Bet. Throughout scripture, a significant few, ordained by the hand of G-d, defeated mighty armies in His *Name*. It took only a few ships to expose and overcome the mighty British-Arab alliance – a Jew for Oil alliance hell-bent on defying the Will of G-d!

Allied hypocrisy did not end with the surrender of Nazi Germany. The clandestine activities of the Aliyah Bet, implemented to circumvent United States and British immigration policies, continued. These clandestine activities were "illegal" according to British (and the U.S. State Department) because they did not adhere to the immigration policies of British/American politicians.

May history bear record, no doubt the Lord has, that the very intelligence agencies of both the United States and Great Britain, who pursued and persecuted those of the clandestine Aliyah Bet movement, were conducting their very own clandestine activities with the remnant of Nazi Germany!!!

After the war, the governments of America (and Great Britain) secretly immigrated thousands, and I mean THOUSANDS of Nazi collaborators and their families into America, filling the job quotas that "DID NOT EXIST" according to Roosevelt and his State Department, and all for the sake of what ... scientific progress, intelligence, military weaponry, industry, banking ...[146] In 1973, Representative Elizabeth Holtzman (founder of the Office of Special Investigation) found government records in the National Archives listing thousands of **Nazis and their families** the Office of Immigration allowed into the United States and work in the Banking System, American industry, and NASA at no consequence!!!

Who would guess that much of the technology and space exploration America has savored, as a result of Project Paperclip, was at the expense of indifference and the righteous blood of butchered, Jewish refugees? The G-d I serve would have adopted both: the innocent, "non-collaborating" scientist, and the Jew. Please excuse me if I paraphrase the words the Christian "messiah" spoke on this wise: *"The foolish do not understand the words I speak, nor can they, for their hearts* [Christian Edomites and Arab Ishmaelites] *are hardened to the simple truth of **love thy neighbor** [the Jews] **as thyself;**"* and would you believe it ... he was a Jew!

The present crisis in Jerusalem would not be a problem if Israel itself and the nations of the world would acknowledge that the one true G-d is "the G-d of Israel" and would submit to His plans for His chosen people. Instead, world political and religious leaders continue to defy G-d, determined to force their agenda upon Israel. That policy can only lead ultimately to Armageddon and G-d's judgment upon this world – and it will.

Christian author Dave Hunt
The Battle for Jerusalem

The Prophet Obadiah

The only Prophet that was a converted Jew. He spoke against the nations
that stood by and did nothing to help Israel in the day of their calamity.

*1:13 You should not have entered into the gate of My people in the
day of their calamity; nor should you have been among those who
looked on their affliction in the day of their calamity; nor have
laid hands on their wealth in the day of their calamity.*

*1:14 And you should not have stood on the crossway to cut down
his fugitives; nor should you have closed in (betrayed) his
remnants in the day of distress.*

*1:15 For the day of the Lord is at hand against all the nations; as
you have done, so shall it be done to you; your due (recompense)
will return upon your own head.*

"Some say the prophecy of Obadiah pertains to the day of retribution, not only
'against all the nations' that wronged Israel in our generation. It also refers to the
years 1939-1945, when the Germans put into operation their plan to exterminate
the Jews completely. In part they succeeded in achieving their purpose. During
that time, the nations 'stood on the crossway to cut down' those who managed to
escape [and stole their property]. They 'closed in' the refugees and either
interned them in camps or forced them to return to their countries of origin. They
also betrayed the refugees who managed to reach ports of haven. Nor did they
do everything in their power to prevent the killing of Jews [American Jewish
Congress, State Department, Jewish Agency]. May G-d avenge the blood of our
brothers!"[147]

Ben Hecht

The fact of the matter is that Roosevelt and his State
Department, the American and Palestinian Zionists all
turned their backs on the European Jews. Perhaps there is
nothing hypocritical about befriending politicians who
supported the very regime that murdered millions of

innocent people, including the Jews who were barred from migrating into North and South America and their G-d given homeland. Any person or nation that values quotas more than a human soul, that persistently challenges the Will of G-d, who denies Israel their G-d given land, whose arrogant spirit whole-heartedly embraces the god of indifference, who robs and steals from his neighbor, is destined to answer the call of pestilence, diseases, and natural disasters.

What can and should be said of the British in charge of Palestine, unlike the powers to be in America and the Jewish Agency, is that, tortuously, they were instrumental in "saving" some 56,000 Aliyah Bet refugees (on Cyprus) and as many in the Atlit camp in Palestine ... who would all eventually become citizens of Israel!

* * *

Often, I find myself sitting in my workshop unaware of the events taking place right before my very eyes. What voyage, what solace awaits me tomorrow as I begin constructing my next Aliyah Bet ship? My models, fashioned out of love, compassion, and contrition are a living testimony to the power of words and authors who possess the uncanny ability to reach out and meld our souls into one. It is one thing to pass the time away thinking about what you have read, it is an entirely different matter relinquishing part of your soul to those thoughts; and that is precisely what transpires each and every time I construct an Aliyah Bet ship!

It was the Lord who handpicked the Aliyah Bet ships for the glory of His *Name*. That being said, it is comforting to know that somewhere in the framework of time and space, as a memorial to Israel, is a fleet of Aliyah Bet models destined to be formed and fitted by the Master's hand; and I, no doubt, will gladly assist.

You are all welcome to Marfa, Texas and visit my Aliyah Bet Museum.

"Your museum of Aliyah Bet ships is the only Holocaust Museum of its kind in the world. What a wonderful blessing!"

The Dallas Holocaust Museum

Part of my ongoing collection of Aliyah Bet ships all of which were destroyed by the British after WWII. All my models are constructed from my own plans taken from surviving photographs. The models are plank-on-frame models using a variety of hard woods. Several of these models are one-of-a-kind and all historically significant. This is not the last time the Lord will use a fleet of ships to bring his chosen back to Israel.

The Question

Hundreds of "secular" Jews and Gentiles have visited my museum, all of which never heard of the Aliyah Bet. The overwhelming question that mystified these inquiring souls was/is *why* ... why have the nations of the world contended with Israel since their inception on Mt. Sinai? The G-d of Israel specifically addresses this question throughout the Jewish scriptures.

Contrary to the whims of Gentile scholarship, Moses received <u>two</u> laws on Mt. Sinai as the *Torah* clearly states. G-d further stated that the Gentiles will succeed in altering his Written Law (the "Old Testament" of the Christian Bible), but would not be able to alter His Oral Law - His primary Law! Consequently, the nations of the world would profess that there was no Oral Law given on Mt. Sinai ... precisely what Pauline Christianity professes today.

All things of G-d are written in parallel verse throughout the Hebrew scriptures. This is accomplished via "alternation and introversion" of biblical passages referred to as the Law of Correspondence. All the scientific laws known to mankind are an exact replica of this Hebraic, Creation Law – a Law that cannot be altered by Gentile Scholars. The following is a small sample of Hebraic parallelism (all are *these two become one* parallels):

Wisdom	Understanding
Father	Holy Spirit
Writing	Arithmetic
Written Law	Oral Law
Body	Spirit
Counting	Measuring

Something unique transpired during the destruction of the two Jewish Temples, the crusades, the inquisitions, the multitude of pogroms against Jews, the 1242 "burning" of Notre Dame, and the Holocaust (to name a few). All these events began with the destruction of every sacred *Torah* (Written Law) and *Talmud* (Oral Law) the Gentiles could get their hands on.

These texts took years to write and only seconds to destroy. Not only do Gentile scholars alter the Lord's sacred texts, they also try to destroy all that He wrote. In 1242, the Priests of Notre Dame gathered 1200 Talmudic texts and burned them in the Notre Dame Square and forced the Jews to convert or be killed. What did the Nazis burn on Kristallnacht? The Babylonians, the Greeks, the Romans all destroyed the Jews sacred texts and forbade them from writing more.

The *Talmud* (Oral Law) was written in 500 C.E.. Why did it take the Gentiles so long to question its validity?? The 70 nations of the world during the time of Moses were offered the *Torah* (by G-d) and rejected His Law. The nations of the world today still reject His Law (as did Paul) and will continue to do so until the arrival of the Messiah when, according to Jewish scriptures, all nations will not only embrace the Law, but will also keep the Lord's 7th Day Sabbath (Written Law) and the festival of Sukkot (as prescribed in the Oral Law) – neither festival was ever created, hence, can never be "done away with."

"It is true we are barbarians. It is an honorable title to us. I am freeing humanity from a false vision called conscience and morality. The Jews have inflicted two wounds on mankind – circumcision (Mosaic/Oral Law) on its body and conscious on its soul (Written Law). The war for world domination will be fought entirely between us, the Germans, and the Jews. All else is façade."

Hitler

So, ... there is your "why."

119

The Land of Israel

According to the writings of the Sages, the Lord provided each nation (70 in all) a guardian angel, but Moses specifically asked that G-d Himself (not an angel) protect Israel and the Lord honored Moses. A study of the 6-Day War would convince the most ardent skeptic that the Lord still honors His commitment to Moses, Israel, and the *Torah*.

I can still recall my father and me listening to the TV commentators as they monitored the Israeli/Arab conflict of 1967. Israel was surrounded by Egypt, Jordan, Iraq, and Syria. On the 6th day of the war all ended abruptly. Even the commentators were unaware as to what had transpired, confused, and unable to explain what the entire world witnessed the morning of the 7th day. No other nation in my lifetime can boast of the power of divine intervention including miracles of biblical proportion, reminiscent of the days when the Lord destroyed the Philistine and Assyrian armies.

I witnessed thousands of Arabic soldiers leave their tanks, military vehicles, and walk home. They were sure to discard their weapons, ammunition, and supplies. The Jordanian army also had left Jerusalem and returned to their homeland without vehicles, weapons, and military supplies. When captured by the Israelis, the Jordanian General simply raised his hand toward Jerusalem. When asked why his army left their military weapons of war in the streets of Jerusalem, his response was that in the early morning, his army saw the "hand of G-d" in the sky and He (G-d) spoke to the entire Jordanian army saying "leave my people alone!"

The Syrian and Egyptian armies saw and heard the call from G-d to leave His people alone.[148] These armies also witnessed thousands of angels dressed in white uniforms on white horses surrounding Jerusalem and documented such. "We will fight the Israelis to the death, but not the angels of G-d."[149] The PBS commentators interviewed these very soldiers concerning their encounter with the angels of G-d. Divine intervention such as witnessed during the 6-Day War has accompanied Israel with each and every war Israel has encountered with these Arabic nations since 1948.

Recall what Moses said to Israel prior to their entering the land of Canaan. Those who bless Israel will be blessed and those who curse Israel will be cursed (especially those who desire to see Jerusalem divided and those determined to prevent Israel from occupying their entire G-d given land). According to scripture, His covenant with Israel is eternal, and His *Torah* prophecies have yet come to their full fruition. It was Joshua who led the nation of Israel on their conquest of Canaan. He was to destroy all seven nations (remnant of the Nephilim). The Lord was displeased with Joshua for he failed to conquer all the land of Canaan. To this very day, the three areas Joshua disobeyed and left intact were/are the Golan Heights, the Gaza Strip, and the West Bank. The Lord was sure to inform Joshua that these areas would forever burden Israel – and they have.

The Palestinian terrorists have never ceased sending rockets and firebombs to kill Jewish citizens (the original Palestinians) while the rest of the world condemns Israel for defending themselves and killing Palestinian civilians placed in arms way by Hamas terrorists. The Palestinian Arabs living in Israel today, refugees of past Arab genocides, were adopted into Israel and now seek to destroy those who provided them safe haven. The Lord foretold this.

The original "Palestinians" were 100% Jews! When the Romans conquered Israel, they renamed the land Palestine and all its occupants (Jews) Palestinians.

Notes

---

[1] Utilizing Paul Silverstone lists 1 and 2, and cross checking with Dalia Ofer's Appendix G list in *Escaping the Holocaust*, there are 144 private and Aliyah ships listed.

[2] "Aliyah Bet," Wikipedia, p. 2.

[3] Bauer, Yehuda. *Jews for Sale* (Yale University Press, 1994), p.35.

[4] Most, if not all of these Nuremberg Laws, including disallowing Jews to enlist in the German military, are in line with the Lord's covenant with the Jews – especially assimilation of Jews with the nations.

[5] Cymet, David. *History vs. Apologetics: The Holocaust, the Third Reich, and the Catholic Church* (Lexington Books, 2012), p. 128.

[6] Rabbi Shmuel Yerushalmi. *The Torah Anthology: The Book of Tehillim* (New York: Moznaim Publishing Corp., 1990), pp. 130, 131.

[7] William R. Perl (December 1, 1989). *The Holocaust conspiracy: an international policy of genocide*, SP Books. pp. 37-. ISBN 978-0-944007-24-2.

[8] Ronnie S. Landau (2006). *The Nazi Holocaust*. I.B. Tauris. pp. 137-140. ISBN 978-1-84511-201-1. Retrieved 24 March 2011.

[9] Klüger, Ruth. *The Secret Ship* (New York: Doubleday & Company, 1978), pp. 77-78.

[10] Ibid, p. 89.

[11] New York Times: "Evian and Geneva" by Walter F. Mondale, 1979.

[12] Herb Karliner was aboard the MS St. Louis in 1939. In his possession is a small booklet, a reprinting of Captain Schroder's original German diary of the St. Louis voyage where he quotes: "The Coast Guard and planes came close, and stopped us from landing at the Port of Miami." *The Jerusalem Post* article dated April 24, 2014.

[13] In 2018, the Canadian Prime Minister Justin Trudeau apologized for his nations decision to disallow a safe haven for the Jewish refugees aboard the M. S. St Louis.

[14] Quoted from *So Near, and Yet So Far: Klara's Voyage on the MS St. Louis*. Chabad-Lubavitch of Westboro's Jewish Youth Library, Ottawa, Canada. Article from Chabad.org by Sara Trappler-Spielman dated February 6, 2012.

[15] "*Historian: New evidence shows FDR's Bigotry derailed many holocaust rescue plans,*" Article by Matt Lebovic, The Times of Israel. The Jews Should Keep Quiet, Published in September through The Jewish Publication Society, Medoff's book includes new archival materials about the relationship between Roosevelt and Rabbi Stephen Wise, who the author sees as a sycophantic Jewish leader used by Roosevelt to "keep the Jews quiet." In his book about Franklin Roosevelt

and the Holocaust, Rafael Medoff finds links between the US president's anti-Japanese stances and his policies against Jews fleeing Hitler.

[16] Cymet, David. *History vs. Apologetics: The Holocaust, the Third Reich, and the Catholic Church* , p. 129.

[17] "Kristallnacht and the World's Response," reprint from The Jewish Week.

[18] *Mississippi History Now*, "German Prisoners of War in Mississippi" by John Skates, 1943-1946, p. 3. And, *World Association of International Studies*, "Ike and German POWs in WWII" by John Eipper, September 2014.

[19] Holocaust Encyclopedia, "Seeking Refuge in Cuba, 1939."

[20] Ibid.

[21] The Library of Congress, "111th Congress 2009, Senate Resolution 111.

[22] *Manchester Guardian*. 24 May 1939, p. 8.

[23] Ho describes his diplomatic career in *My Forty Years as a Diplomat* (Pittsburgh, PA: Dorrance Publishing Co., 2010), translated and edited by his son Monto Ho.

[24] Yukiko Sugihara (1995), *Visas for Life*. Edu-Comm Plus. ISBN 0-9649674-0-5. Wikipedia: "Chiune Sugihara."

[25] Alex Grobman and Daniel Landers (ed.), *Genocide, Critical Issues of the Holocaust* (Los Angeles, 1983, p. 299.

[26] D.S. Pitts, "Central European Jews – Arrival in Shanghai," March 15, 1939, D5422(c), SMP files; letter of March 28, 1939, from the secretary of the Municipal Council to the Commissioner of Police, D5422(c), SMP files.

[27] Gerhard Krebs, "Antisemitismus and Judenpolitik der Japaner," in *Exil Shanghai 1938-1947*, ed. Armbrüster, Kohlstruck, and Mühlberger, pp. 65-66.

[28] "The Refugee Problem," North China Herald, December 28, 1938, p. 529; Cordell Hull's telegram to U.S. Embassy in Berlin, archived in United States National Archives, file number 893.55J/4, microfilm publication LM63, roll 143. Reprinted in Steve Hochstadt, *Source of the Holocaust* (Houndmills, UK, and New York: Palgrave Macmillian, 2004), p. 83.

[29] Marvin Tokayer and Mary Swartz, *The Fugu Plan, The Untold Story of the Japanese and Jews during World War II* (New York and London, 1979, p. 223.

[30] Klüger, Ruth. *The Secret Ship* (New York: Doubleday & Company, 1973), p. 119. ISBN: 0-385-11328-5.

[31] Shillony, Ben-Ami. *The Jews and the Japanese: The Successful Outsiders* (Tokyo: Charles E. Tuttle Company, 1991), p.184.

[32] Tokayer, Marvin; Swartz, Mary (2004-05-31). *The Fugu Plan: The Untold Story of the Japanese and the Jews During World War II.* Gefen Publishing House Ltd.

[33] Wikipedia, "1929 Hebron Massacre."

[34] Genesis 12:3. Throughout the Torah, G-d warned the house of Jacob not to harm their brother the Edomite nations (Esau) including Rome, Europe, and the USA (written in Hebrew and reversed spells EDOM). Ever since Israel left Egypt, the Edomite nations have sought out and killed millions of the Lord's chosen people including the Native Indians in North and South America (possibly part of the lost ten tribes of Israel). The Lord told Moses that when the Messiah is come, the Lord Himself will judge these Edomite nations. Woe to the Christian missionaries whose goal it is to convert Orthodox Jews to their heathen religion of Baal – professing a man to be G-d.

[35] "The Holocaust in Romania" (PDF). Bucharest, Romania: International Commission on the Holocaust in Romania. November 11, 2004.

[36] The History Place: Holocaust Timeline.

[37] Jewish Virtual Library. The Holocaust: The Mufti's Conversation with Hitler pledging to keep Jews out of Palestine and assisted Hitler with the "final solution" of the Jews. In concert with Hitler, Britain (and Russia) signed the 1942 Iran Oil Treaty aligning itself with the Muslim nations in keeping Jews out of Palestine. Britain has a choice, Jew, Oil, or Jew and Oil, they chose JEW and OIL!! It was also in 1942 when the "Refrom" Jewish Congress, Roosevelt, and Secretary of State Cordell Hall suppressed information on "mobile gas chambers and mass shootings of Jews in Poland." Rabbi Wise knew that the government could facilitate rescue efforts, but he "rarely pushed Roosevelt and this gave the administration the option to ignore Jewish pressure without fear of political retribution or public controversy." (Urofsky, *A Voice That Spoke for Justice*, pp. 322-327.) Supply ships to England returned empty when that could have brought refugees – in 1943, 200,000 German and Italian POW's were brought by these ships to detention camps in America, but no JEWS. Rapoport, Shake Heaven and Earth (Gefen Publishing House, 1000), pp. 70/71.

You have heard about the many opportunities American and British bombers could have bombed Nazi extermination camps but chose not to prioritize the issue. Not one journalist, war correspondent, politician, or historian has ever ventured to TELL THE TRUTH!!! The truth of the matter is that the "Jew for Oil" was (and still is) in effect!!! America and Great Britain will always choose Oil over the Lord's chosen people.

[38] Klüger, Ruth. *The Secret Ship*, p. 119.

[39] Their Voices Live On: "57 Days of Hell — The Voyage of HMT Dunera, 1940."

[40] Byers, Ann. Saving Children from the Holocaust (Berkeley Heights: Enslow Publishers, Inc., 2012), pp. 96-98.

[41] Bartrop, Paul. *The Dunera Affair* (Melbourne: Schwartz & Wilkinson, 1990), p. 189.

[42] Wikipedia. HMT Dunera.

[43] Klüger, Ruth. pp. 37-38.

[44] 2all.co.il: "Pentcho – Symbol of the Rescue Immigration."

[45] *Yad Edinetz*, The Edinetz Association, 1973, Tel Aviv.

[46] JewishGen. Romanis SIG: "The Struma Tragedy."

[47] Szulc, Tad. *The Secret Alliance: The Extraordinary Story of the Rescue of the Jews Since World War II* (London: Pan Books, 1992), p.31. ISBN: 978-0-374-24946-5. Also, Ynet news.com article by Baruch Cohen: "Well-kept secret: Romania's sale of Jews following World War II remains one of the 20th century's least-reported stories" (5/23/2005).

[48] Klüger, Ruth. p. 95.

[49] Ofer, Dalia. Escaping the Holocaust (New York: Oxford University Press, 1990), p. 162.

[50] Moyne to Law, December 24, 1941. PRO CO 733/449/P3/4/30. Cited in Wasserstein, Britain, pp. 145-146; also see High Commissioner, Jerusalem, to Colonial Office, December 22, 1941.

[51] Think-Israel. "The Blockade: How The British Prevented Rescue by David Krakow." This was posted February 18, 2009 on MidEast Truth Forum. http://mideasttruth.com/forum/viewtopic.php?t=8963

[52] Wymann, David. *The Abandonment of the Jews: America and the Holocaust 1941-45* (New York: Pantheon Books, 1984), p. 179.

[53] Sidney Zion. "Book Skewers FDR Inaction on Eurpoe's Jews," *New York Daily News*, September 21, 1999. Also, The History Place: Holocaust Timeline: "… all 70,000 perished."

[54] Friedman, Saul. *No Haven for the Oppressed*, p. 150.

[55] Aiken, Lisa. *Why Me G-d: A Jewish Guide for Coping and Suffering* (Amherst: AeroType, Inc., 1997), p. 235.

[56] De Wever, Bruno. *Local government in occupied Europe: (1939-1945)* (Gent: Academia Press, 2006), p.206. ISBN: 978-90-382-0892-3.

[57] Morse, Arthur. *While Six Million Died: A Chronicle of American Apathy* (New York: The Overlook Press, 1998), p. 40.

[58] Yad Yashem. Shoah Resource Center, The International School for Holocaust Studies, "Shanghai." (www.yadvashem.org)

⁵⁹ Think-Israel. David Krakow. "More than 50 years later, it was finally learned that the British had cracked the German code and tracked the murders of the Jews in the summer of 1941 as they were being reported to Berlin in coded messages used by the German commanders of the SS and police units carrying out the "executions." This was established by Prof. Richard Breitman of American University in Washington (and other scholars) who had requested the declassification of 1.3 million wartime documents from the National Security Agency under the Freedom of Information Act. The documents that were subsequently released to the National Archives included 282 pages of SS radio intercepts."

⁶⁰ Wymann, David, p. 29.

⁶¹ Rapoport, Louis. *Shake Heaven & Earth* (Jerusalem: Gefen Publishing House, 1999), pp. 95-98.

⁶² Goldmann autoed in State Department Memorandum 867 N. 01/2347.

⁶³ Tad Szulc. The Secret Aliance (New York, Farrar, Straus & Giroux, 1991), p. 11.

⁶⁴ Rapoport, op. cit., p. 102.

⁶⁵ Rapoport, op. cit., p. 92.

⁶⁶ Ibid, p. 90.

⁶⁷ Morse, Arthur, p. 52.

⁶⁸ Internet: Jewish Virtual Library. "Holocaust Rescue: Rescue of Danish Jews."

⁶⁹ Ibid.

⁷⁰ Some years ago, the late Dr. Meir Rosenne, who served as Israel's ambassador to France and to the United States, and also as the Foreign Ministry's chief legal adviser, suggested that the Jewish state has a legal right and duty to demand the return of cultural objects that were stolen from Jews during World War II and over the centuries (original books, manuscripts, sacred objects, and art). These are currently being stored in basements, libraries and museums around the world, like those detained by the Catholic Church and the Prague Jewish Museum, where the Nazis first stored materials and objects from the destroyed Jewish communities. The Vatican still hasn't returned to the Jewish state a number of artifacts that belong to the Jewish people, including several books, manuscripts, Torah scrolls, Talmuds and one Temple candelabra given to Pope Innocent III. *"Time to Return Nazi-looted art,"* Jewish News Syndicate, January 31, 2020.

On August 17, 2021, the Polish government declassified Holocaust files detailing land and treasures stolen from Polish Jews during WWII. When asked to return Jewish property, the Polish government was sure to deny their request. Stealing from your neighbor is a serious offence against God – the very sin that brought about the biblical flood!

[71] Internet: JewishGen, "The Sinking of the Mefkure" by Rosanne Leeson.

[72] Jacobs, Benjamin. *The 100-Year Secret* (Guilford: The Lyons Press, 2004), p. 83.

[73] Jacobs, Benjamin. *The 100-Year Secret*, p. 72.

[74] Jacobs, Benjamin. *The 100-Year Secret*, p. 97.

[75] Ibid., p. 76.

[76] Ibid., p. 170.

[77] The Nizkor Project. "The Dentist of Auschwitz," Chapter 18: *Inferno*.

[78] "It was falsely reported that the Nazi leadership planned to move to Norway and to fight on from there having assembled around 500 ships in Lübeck Bay and Kiel Bay for this purpose. This falsehood remains uncorrected in English publication until today." Bert Intres, survivor of the *Cap Arcona*, 1995.

[79] Vaughan, Hal (2004). *Doctor to the Resistance: The Heroic True Story of an American Surgeon and His Family in Occupied Paris.* Brassey's. pp. 148, 154-57. ISBN: 1-57488-773-4. Jacobs, Benjamin. *The 100-Year Secret*, p. 161, 162. Bond, D.G. (1993). *German history and German identity: Uwe Johnson's Jahrestage. Rodopi*, pp. 150-151. ISBN: 90-5183-459-4.

[80] Jacobs, Benjamin. *The 100-Year Secret*, p. 175-176.

[81] Jacobs, Benjamin. *The 100-Year Secret*, p. 173.

[82] Jacobs, Benjamin. *The 100-Year Secret*, p. 179.

[83] Louis Rapoport, *Shake Heaven & Earth*, (Gefen Publishing House, 1999), p.39.

[84] Hecht, Ben. *Perfidy,* (Gefen Publishing House, 1999). The Jewish Agency did succeed in bartering throughout the war a few thousand of "elitist" Jews including 1200 Hungarian Jews with the help of Adolf Eichmann. As for the other 800,000 Hungarian Jews, the Agency told Eichmann that "he could have the others" (Eichmann Confessions, p. 261). Fortunately, several of the abandoned Hungarian Jews, on their way to Auschwitz, escaped to tell who and how the Jewish Agency conspired with Eichmann to rid Europe of their remaining Jews (p. 105).

"It is enough for us that a Jewish man (Kastner of the Jewish Agency), an ex-Zionist leader, dared to recommend mercy, almost in the name of the whole Jewish people, for one of the major sharks of the German war criminals before the authorities who detained him, and to cause, alone or together with others, the release and evasion of punishment of this great criminal." Supreme Court Judge Silberg.

Rudolf Kastner of the Jewish Agency provided the Nazi criminal Kurt Becker the funds to flee to Argentina. Becker assisted the Agency in securing the murder of thousands of European Jewish refugees. (Read Ben Hecht's book _Perfidy_ for all the details recorded in Israeli courts.) [85] Evidence testifying to thie sorture technique was given during the Civil Case of Paul Kollek v. Herut (Civil Case No. 503/49 in the District Court of Tel Aviv).

[86] Ben-Gurion was a secular Jew and fought for the establishment of a Jewish nation void of Jewish religious traditions and the Torah. His Jewish Agency that controls Israel immigration today (whose Chief Officer is Adolph Kastner's Daughter) has allowed very few, if any, religious Orthodox Jews to aliyah into their homeland since the end of WWII! This agency is also actively involved with the Messianic community in Israel converting Orthodox Jews to Christianity. The Jewish scriptures (Tanach) is very specific as to what will become of those Jews who forsake the Lord's Torah, three-quarters of all Jews upon the arrival of the Messiah will be destroyed for abandoning his Torah.

[87] Rapoport, op. cit., p. 207.

[88] Hecht. _Perfidy_, p. 37.

[89] Ibid.

[90] Ibid.

[91] Rapoport, op. cit., p.206.

[92] Hecht, _Perfidy_, pp. 38, 39.

[93] Ibid. pp.38-40. Today's Israel Government history books teach the children of the land that Jaffa was captured by the Jewish Agency Haganah when, in fact, it was through the intervention (against the Agency's order) of Menachem Begin and his army of less than one thousand men and women who stormed and captured the city of Jaffa. When the battle-worn Palmach and Irgun stood in the hills of Jerusalem holding off the Arabs, Ben-Gurion assured the U.N. that his new government **doesn't want Jerusalem**, and cravenly agreed to "internationalize" the Old City (p. 39).

[94] Ibid. 40-41.

[95] This book gives new meaning to the phrase "cult classic." Published in the early 1960's it deals with one of the great "cause celebres" in Israeli history – the Kastner Affair – which remains almost wholly unknown in the English speaking world. To this very day, public aring of this controversy in English is discouraged.

[96] Hecht. _Perfidy_, p. iii.

[97] Ibid, p.261.

[98] Harrison, Earl G. _Report of Earl G. Harrison_ (The Jewish Student Online Research Center-JSOURCE) From _Truman's Letter Regarding_

the *Harrison Repor t on the Treatment of Displaced Jews*, p. 5. Internet: http://www.us-israel.org/jsource/holocaust/dptoc.html

[99] Harrison, p. 4.

[100] Yehudit Kleiman and Nina Springer-Aharoni, eds., *The Anguish of Liberation: Testimonies From 1945* (Jerusalem: Yad Vashem, 1995), p.53.

[101] Ibid, p. 58.

[102] Nasaw, David. *The Last Million* (Penguin Press, N.Y., 2020), p.72.

[103] Ibid, p. 71.

[104] Gottfried, Ted. *Displaced Persons: The Liberation and Abuse of Holocaust Survivors* (Brookfield: Twenty-First Century Books, 2001), p. 62. Initially lacking sufficient manpower, the British allowed the Hungarians to remain in charge and only commandant Kramer was arrested. Subsequently SS and Hungarian guards shot and killed some of the starving prisoners who were trying to get their hands on food supplies from the store houses. Knoch, Habbo (ed) (2010). *Bergen-Belsen: Wehrmacht POW Camp 1940–1945, Concentration Camp 1943–1945, Displaced Persons Camp 1945–1950. Catalogue of the permanent exhibition*. Wallstein. ISBN 978-3-8353-0794-0. The Poles on the National Committees were formerly executioners for the SS, were anti-Semitic, and discriminated against the Jews in so far as rations and clothes and general treatment. Nasaw. *The Last Million*, pp. 69,70.

[105] Nasaw. *The Last Million*, p. 66.

[106] Shandler, Jeffery. While America Watches: Televising the Holocaust (New York: Oxford University Press, 1999), p. 11; "Nazi Murder Mills, April 26, 1945 Universal Newsreel," YouTube, www.youtube.com/watch?v=8jdefO0Dxhc&bpctr=1577134762.

[107] Gottfried, Ted. p. 62.

[108] *Memo to America: The DP Story*, p. 11.

[109] Gottfried, Ted. p. 35.

[110] Sachar, Howard. *A History of the Jews in America* (New York: Alfred A. Knopf, 1992), p. 555.

[111] The Jewish Student Online Research Center (JSOURCE) *Truman's Letter Regarding the Harrison Report on the Treatment of Displaced Jews*, p. 1,2.

[112] Szulc. The Secret Alliance (New York, Farrar, Straus & Giroux), p. 97.

[113] Sachar, Abram. *The Redemption of the Unwanted* (New York: St. Martin/Marek, 1983), p. 165.

[114] *Comptom's Interactive Encyclopedia*, 1998.

[115] Sachar, Abram. p. 163.

[116] Academy Award-winning documentary film directed by Mark Jonathan Harris, The Long Way Home (First Run Features, 1997).

Exerpts from Patton's letters and diaries found in "The Patton Papers" collected by Martin Blumenson, a military historian.

[117] Letter to wife Beatrice, September 2, 1945.

[118] Luther's sentiments were widely echoed in the Germany of the 1930s, particularly within the Nazi party. Hitler's Education Minister, Bernhard Rust, was quoted by the *Völkischer Beobachter* as saying that: "Since Martin Luther closed his eyes, no such son of our people has appeared again. It has been decided that we shall be the first to witness his reappearance ... I think the time is past when one may not say the names of Hitler and Luther in the same breath. They belong together; they are of the same old stamp [*Schrot und Korn*]". *Völkischer Beobachter*, August 25, 1933 cited in Steigmann-Gall, Richard. *The Holy Reich: Nazi Conceptions of Christianity*, 1991–1945. Cambridge University Press, 2003, pp. 136–7. ISBN: 0-521-82371-4.

Luther is renowned still today as the initiator and leader of the Protestant Reformation. Centuries later, Lutherans and Germans alike admire and honor him for his bold and daring actions against the Catholic Church in the 1500s. The pervasive portrayal of Luther is simple; the young, impassioned monk who took on the Roman Catholic Church and won. However, Luther is much more complex, with a darker side that is much less well-known. Hitler remains one of the most hated men in history. Sometimes referred to as an evil genius, but mostly just evil, Hitler is more notorious than celebrated. Hitler was adept at hiding who he really was; he was careful not to let people get too close, to see behind the façade. Protestant Christians were careful to let only Luther's legacy live on, while downplaying the less favorable version. While there is no hiding the evil that occurred under Hitler's reign, the sinister side of Luther has been well-hidden since his time, allowing only his enlightened and reformist persona to be remembered and hailed. Many people would be surprised to find out that Martin Luther was extraordinarily anti-Judaic, becoming increasingly more vile as he aged. Wanting early on to convert the Jews so that they can be saved by Christ, Luther took their refusal personally and eventually became consumed with bitter hatred. This rage eventually led to texts and sermons that explicitly detailed why the Jews were wicked and what should be done with them. Was this normal behavior for Luther's time, or were his views considered extreme? One might even argue that there is little difference between the anti-Semitic ideologies of Martin Luther and Adolf Hitler. *Luther and Hitler: A Linear Connection between Martin Luther and Adolf Hitler's Anti-Semitism with a Nationalistic Foundation Daphne M. Olsen,* December 2011 Rollins College Hamilton Holt School Master of Liberal Studies Program Winter Park, Florida.

[119] Sherman, Franklin. *Faith Transformed: Christian Encounters with Jews and Judaism*, edited by John Merkle, (Collegeville, Minnesota: Liturgical Press, 2003), pp. 63, 64.

[120] Gottfried, Ted. p. 40.

[121] The biblical Edomite nations include the daughters of Rome, namely: the Vatican, Italy, France, Germany, England, and America. Rome was established by Edomites (Constantine being the Head Edomite), not the Edomites that converted to Judaism in the Second Century, but those that had not converted in the First Century. This is also confirmed by the Protestant Church who split from the Roman Catholic, Edomite Church.

[122] Szulc, Tad. *The Secret Alliance*, p. 129.

[123] Holocaust Encyclopedia. "The Kielce Pogrom: A Blood Libel Massacre of Holocaust Survivors."

[124] William H. Honan, "Rudolph Patzert, 88; Transported Jews to Palestine After War," Obituary in *The New York Times*, February 21, 2000, p. A 17.

[125] Wikipedia: Mossad LeAliyah Bet. Hochstein, Joseph. *The Jews Secret Fleet* (New York: Gefen Publishing House Ltd., 1987), p. xii.

[126] Hunt, David. 'The Battle For Jerusalem, Chapter 6 of *The Gathering Storm* (Springfield: 21st Century Press, 2005), p. 129.

[127] Sachar, Abram. *The Redemption of the Unwanted*, p. 157.

[128] Ibid., p. 183.

[129] Eliav, Arie. *The Voyage of the Ulua* (New York: Funk and Wagnalls, 1969), p. 166.

[130] Hochstein, Joseph. *The Jews Secret Fleet* (New York: Gefen Publishing House Ltd., 1987), p. 127.

[131] Ibid., p. 128.

[132] Ibid.

[133] Cohen, Michael J. *Palestine and the Great Powers 1945–1948* (Princeton, 1982), pp. 254-255, and Aviva Halamish, *Exodus: The Real Story* [Hebrew] (Tel Aviv, 1990), pp. 133–34.

[134] Ben-Gurion addressing UNSCOP on July 4, 1947.

[135] Hunt, David, p. 129.

"Events transpiring in the Middle East relative to Israel and making today's headlines are not chance occurrences but precise fulfillments of what G-d through His Hebrew prophets foretold for these 'last days.' Each day's news adds fresh proof that the biblical G-d is the one true G-d and that the Bible alone is His inspired Word to mankind. We see unfolding before us precisely what G-d said He would cause Israel and the nations around her to experience. In one of the most awesome and frightening prophecies for the future, G-d declares, 'I will gather all the nations [and He means all] against Jerusalem to battle, and the city will be captured... Then the LORD will go forth and fight against those nations...' (Zech 14:1-3). When this will occur we do not know - but as events in the Middle East come to a climax, we may be certain that ultimately a world that is in defiance of G-d in so many ways, not the least of which is its attitude toward Israel, is headed for the fulfillment of this prophecy."

[136] Sachar, Howard. p. 602.

[137] The Daily Beast article entitled "Exclusive WW2 Britain Blew Up Jewish Refugee Ships" by Andrew Roberts. Reference to Keith Jeffery book *The Secret History of MI6*, pp. 689-692.

[138] Jeffrey, Keith. *The Secret History of MI6* (New York: The Penguin Press, 2010), pp.688-697.

[139] Wikipedia: Aliyah Bet.

[140] Wikipedia: Ho Feng-Shan and Chiune Sugihara.

[141] Wikipedia: Gustav Schröder.

[142] According to the Jewish Sages, the Egyptian "three days of darkness" began with the deaths of four-fifths (12 million) of the descendants of Jacob who chose to assimilate among the Egyptian people. Also, in **Deuteronomy 31:16-18, the word "Holocaust" is spelled out in equal letter spacing of 50 letter increments – placed by the hand of Moses some 3250 years before the Holocaust.**

[143] Jeremiah 16:19.

[144] Jim's WordPress.com site: "What do the Golan Heights, Hebron and the Gaza Strip have in common...and why should we care?"

[145] Ecclesiastes 12:13. Gentiles are required to keep the Seven Laws of Noah including the law against worshipping false gods as did the Baal-god/man worshippers of Canaan. Few Christians have ever heard of the Noahide Laws.

[146] Wikipedia: Operation paperclip.

[147] Hecht, Ben. p. 485.

[148] The War College Library possesses books written by both the Syrian and Jordanian Generals who witnessed these events. Mr. Steven Speights constructed American Embassy's throughout the Mid-East and can personally attest to having read these publications mentioned here.

[149] View the 2-hour PBS 6-Day War documentary on the internet.